Student Engagement is FUNdamental

Building a Learning Community with Hands-on Activities

Jane Feber

**MAUPIN HOUSE BY
CAPSTONE PROFESSIONAL**
a capstone imprint

Student Engagement is FUNdamental: Building a Learning Community with Hands-on Activities
By Jane Feber

Cover design: Studio Montage
Book design: Hank McAfee
Photography: Zachary A. Bennett
Illustrations: Candace Hollinger

Library of Congress Cataloging-in-Publication Data

Feber, Jane, 1951-
  Student engagement is FUNdamental : building a learning community with hands-on activities / by Jane Feber.
    p. cm.
  Includes bibliographical references and indexes.
  ISBN 978-1-936700-47-9
  1. Activity programs in education. 2. Active learning. 3. Motivation in education. 4. Teacher-student relationships. I. Title.
  LB1027.25.F43 2011
  371.33--dc23
                    2011034374

Maupin House publishes professional resources for K-12 educators. Contact us for tailored, in-school training or to schedule an author for a workshop or conference.
Visit www.capstonepd.com for free lesson plan downloads.

Maupin House Publishing, Inc. by Capstone Professional
1710 Roe Crest Drive
North Mankato, MN 56003
www.capstonepd.com
888-262-6135
info@capstonepd.com

A good teacher becomes a better teacher when she has a colleague to act as a sounding board to share ideas, triumphs, and debacles. I dedicate this book to my BFF, Diane Bondurant. She is always there to lend an ear, share her expertise, and suggest a new idea.

And I can't forget my mother. . . She instilled in me the drive to follow my dreams and was always there to encourage me.

And to my husband, Dan, I can't thank you enough for your patience during the many nights you spent alone as I worked away on my manuscript.

Table of Contents

PART 3 - Mini-book and Fortune Teller Templates

Mini-book Templates

Fortune Teller Templates

Resources

Bibliography

"The quality of teacher-student relationships is the keystone for all other aspects of classroom management."

– ROBERT MARZANO, AUTHOR

After thirty-six years as a classroom teacher engaging my students in the learning process with hands-on strategies, I know one thing for certain: when students *do*, they learn.

Student engagement is fundamental to learning. And it makes learning fun, too. Building rapport with engaging, hands-on activities makes it easy to get to know your students. The hands-on activities immediately begin to build a rapport that creates a favorable and supportive climate for learning—one in which students feel safe, respected, and engaged in the learning process. Learning becomes more personal when students are engaged in the learning process.

Hands-on learning has an even more valuable function, however. For after helping you establish a solid rapport with your students, hands-on activities build solid academic skills that continue to engage and delight your learners and make learning painless.

And they are effective. Research supports the value of engaged, active learning with hands-on activities, even in this era of data gathering and high-stakes testing.

Building Rapport

Let's start with rapport—the imperative first step in creating a classroom climate that supports learning. According to Deborah Stipek (*Educational Leadership*, "Relationships Matter," 2006), adolescents work harder for teachers who treat them as individuals and express interest in their personal lives outside school. When a teacher gets to know her students, the students are able to see that she is truly concerned.

And what are the benefits of establishing a close rapport with your students? My experience has shown me that strong teacher/student rapport produces the following positive results:

- Less stress in the classroom

- Increased motivation

- More student engagement with learning

- Improved attendance

- Student success with academics

So how do we begin to establish rapport with our students? Although a teacher's job is not to become personally involved with students, it definitely *is* your job to know your students. As Booker T. Washington once wisely noted, few things help a child more than to place responsibility on him and to let him know he is trusted.

Here are some ways to get your teacher-student relationships off to the best start.

- Be a good listener. Hear what students tell you.

- Be enthusiastic. Enthusiasm is contagious.

- Be positive. A kind word goes a long way.

- Be gentle, yet firm. It's all about being fair.

- Be interested. Know your students' learning styles and interests.

- Be flexible. It's OK to change the plans.

- Make students laugh. Laughter relaxes students.

- Pick your battles. Use confrontation sparingly.

- Keep your composure. Address the issue.

- Get involved. Try inviting students to eat lunch with you now and then. Attend a sporting event in which they participate. Read the stories and poems they write, and listen to the stories of their weekend sagas and dramas with friends.

Building rapport is a process that begins on the very first day of school. And engaging students with hands-on activities facilitates this process. Through engaging, hands-on rapport-building activities, you will learn a lot about your students: likes and dislikes, hobbies and interests, friends and foes, and the conflicts and personal challenges they face.

The hands-on activities in this resource that build rapport also will provide you with a wealth of information about the academic abilities of your students. Among other things, these beginning activities tell you how well students can organize their thoughts in writing, and they provide a glimpse into their mastery of English conventions. As you build rapport, you are also gaining important diagnostic, benchmark information you can use to guide instruction. Best of all, the activities establish that positive and caring learning community that enables inquiry and learning.

The first two weeks of school. During the first two weeks of school, time spent building a community of learners is time well spent. Having the students do activities where you learn about them personally also lets you see how well they write, think, and speak. Evaluating the activities you assign using a simple rubric will provide data for further instruction.

The rapport-building activities need not take a lot of time, and they should begin on day one. I've found that these activities are a great way to break the ice on those first few days when students may be a little timid. And, remember that the time is well spent because the activities serve double duty: to build a climate for learning and to give you a measure of student abilities.

Use this easy-to-follow, reproducible matrix to help you sort and reference the information you will be gathering.

Name	Hobbies	Interests	Likes	Dislikes

After the First Two Weeks

Engaging students in active learning does not end after the first two weeks. It's still fundamental to learning. According to Lyons and Pinnell, no matter how organized your lesson may be, students will learn only when they are engaged (2001).

So, hands-on activities are an important part of academic learning, too. When students are actively engaged, they are able to apply concepts being taught, and the adage "I see and I forget; I hear and I understand; I do and I remember" holds true.

A classroom that uses hands-on activities for rapport and academic skill building provides student-centered education that makes learning personally meaningful. The hands-on activities invite the whole, real lives of children into the classroom (Zemelman, Daniels, & Hyde, 1998). My experience has shown me that engagement allows students to gain a profound grasp of what they learn, to retain that knowledge, and to develop their abilities to transfer what they learn to new contexts and concepts.

Hands-on activities change classroom practices. If you become committed to engaging students with hands-on activities, it may also change your classroom practices. For example, rote memorization or worksheets don't make for engaged learning or foster a sense of relevancy to learning in a world dominated by fascinating and engaging personal technology such as the Internet, video games, and cell phones. Hands-on learning piques student interest and keeps them interested in learning. Because of this, you will probably find yourself allowing more talk and movement and encouraging collaborative learning.

Today, the value of collaborative learning is well documented as a recognized best practice for building twenty-first century skills for future success in college and the workplace. Collaborative learning requires students to not work alone in their seats all day. Instead, they are encouraged to move around the room, consult with peers, and learn how to work together to find, analyze, and manipulate facts into knowledge as they master skills at higher cognitive levels.

The Common Core Standards focus on the need for students to demonstrate their understanding of knowledge and to analyze written material. One vital key to achieving that goal is through producing authentic products that show they know and understand the concepts that have been taught. That's the very definition of an effective hands-on learning product.

Finally, teachers know that one-size teaching does not really fit anyone. The typical classroom today finds ESL students mixing with gifted and special-needs peers. Hands-on activities used for establishing rapport and building academic skills provide an excellent, naturally differentiated approach to learning—and to teaching. Rubrics can easily be created and modified to fit the levels and needs of students, and collaborative learning in pairs or small groups encourages students to teach one another.

In 2009, I retired from full-time teaching to become a consultant and substitute teacher in my district. Knowing my hands-on approach, many teachers now just leave me the name of the story they are reading or the topic of study with a message, "Jane, just do your thing." And I have had the opportunity to do many wonderful "things" with students at all grade levels.

For a second-grade class studying the water cycle, I quickly constructed sixteen little wheels by the time class began. After I reviewed the material, I gave out the wheels. Students illustrated the text as I reread it. They drew clouds at the top of the wheel with rain falling down. At the bottom of the wheel, lakes, streams, and puddles appeared. Near the top, the sun appeared to begin the cycle once again. Then, as I read the material once more, students described each step of the water cycle process in the boxes on the front portion of the wheel. The activity was a huge success.

For a high-school class of struggling readers, the teacher left instructions to work on the vocabulary for *The Canterbury Tales* and to read as much of the selection as time permitted. This was a pretty difficult selection for these readers. To begin, students created simple bumper stickers in order to help them learn their vocabulary words.

Then each student created a Give One/Get One Flip Book (p. 47) for a peer-response activity. I quickly chunked the text for easier comprehension, and students happily completed this interactive, engaging activity. After the activity, students were able to make meaning of the text even though this was a difficult selection.

When you show students you care and work along with them to establish a climate of respect, they will perform to the best of their abilities, and learning will take place. The key is student engagement. Hands-on activities provide that key.

What Is in This Resource

It's easy for students to sit at their desks and look like they're working. It takes effort on everyone's part—teacher and student—to ensure all students are actively engaged in the learning process. This resource will show you how to reap the benefits of hands-on, active learning in your classroom every day.

Student Engagement is FUNdamental supplies you with 12 rapport-building activities and 21 activities for building academic skills. Note that additional academic applications for the rapport builders are listed on each rapport activity.

In addition, you'll find mini-book and fortune teller templates, along with some suggested uses for these versatile and engaging learning tools. Additional engagement activities are included to build active vocabulary acquisition and active reading skills. An index of academic skills matched with the activities and a correlation of the activities to the Common Core Standards are provided in the Resources section.

Engaging Students Independently and in Groups

Students can be engaged in the learning process while working individually to create a product. But even during a solo work period, students should be allowed to discuss what they are doing, get ideas from others, and share their ideas.

When projects are completed, build in some time for students to present their work to the whole class, to small groups, or even to other classes that might be working on the same unit. Work should also be displayed so that all students can benefit from their peers' thinking.

Not all the activities in this resource include rubrics simply because a rubric may not be needed or desired. Of course, most of the activities can be assessed if you like. A simple rubric can provide an excellent way for students to understand project expectations, even if it is not used for formally assessing an individual activity or group product. A separate rubric can be distributed to each group member to evaluate the cooperative working ability of others in the group to complete the task at hand.

How you choose these activities and use them in your classroom is really up to you! They are flexible and adapt to many learning areas. Most will fit into a fifty-minute period, but some activities do suggest longer periods of time. Feel free to adapt them as your needs dictate.

Partners and small groups. Working with a partner can confirm the belief that often two heads are better than one, yet thought should go into partner selection. Here's one place where knowing your students really pays off to match the task with the proper partner.

The partnering process can be as simple as placing half of the students' names in a basket. Those whose names are not in the basket select a partner from the basket. With an uneven number of students, you can become the final partner, or you can add that student to an existing group.

You can also partner students with different ability levels. With a little advance planning, you can, for example, prepare color-coded strips of paper with one student name on each strip. Only the teacher has to know the coding rationale (although students are quick to figure it out). One color, say blue, can represent students who are competent in the area of study; another color, say yellow, can be those who need more help with the content. The teacher then can select one name from each color to work collaboratively.

Selecting random partners by having students draw color-coded Popsicle® sticks, stickers, or cards selected from a deck of cards is another way to group students. If you want two-student groups, just place two each of coded Popsicle sticks, stickers, or cards in a bag. For example, for a class of eighteen students, label eighteen Popsicle sticks one through nine, twice. Students draw and are randomly matched.

When working together, students must understand their approach is not "You do half and I do half of the work," but "We must work together to complete the assigned task." Any grading rubric should reflect the value of work completed collaboratively and not reward work done independently, then merely assembled at the end. Your job is to facilitate by monitoring partners and providing assistance as needed.

Larger groups. Groups of up to five or six students are often necessary when a large amount of material must be reviewed. In this case, students often do split up the work and determine which part of the assignment each one will research, complete, and present to the class. I have found that heterogeneous groups are most effective for this learning configuration.

Interest groups. Assignments often lend themselves to students selecting topics for projects. In this case, you might want to group students according to their interests; for example, students who are interested in sports working together or those who are interested in a particular planet, country, or novel. In this type of group, students like to determine which aspect of the topic they will be responsible for reporting.

A Note about Teacher Modeling

Students need to know you, too. As you introduce the activities, share your own examples: a Personal Website Poster, your Me Bag or Box, a personal Directory entry. You are modeling your expectations for the activity, and you also are revealing your life. I often think I have as much fun creating samples for my students as they have completing the activities.

Engaged and Ready to Learn

Once a classroom bond has been formed and the rules made clear, the classroom climate is ripe for student success. As the teacher learns her students' strengths and weaknesses, it becomes easier to help them learn. In a classroom in which rapport has been established, the students realize the teacher is supportive and available to provide assistance.

In the engaged classroom, your students know they can ask questions and not be ridiculed. They can move freely about the classroom without distracting others and not be told to sit down. You laugh with your students, and you accept each one for who he or she is. Because you know and appreciate each student's interest and concerns, you have created a relaxed classroom atmosphere in which students are free to become involved in their learning. You are teaching to the Common Core Standards and doing your part to prepare students for college and the workplace.

Who could ask for more? Student engagement with hands-on learning activities is, indeed, FUNdamental!

PART ONE

Engaging Activities That Establish Rapport With Students

"There is no excuse to be bored. Sad, yes. Angry, yes. Depressed, yes. Crazy, yes. But there is no excuse for boredom. Ever."

– VIGGO MORTENSEN, ACTOR

A to Z: All About Me

Using the letters of the alphabet, students list various aspects of themselves and their lives.

ACADEMIC APPLICATION:

This activity can be applied to all content areas. Before studying a content topic, students can complete words they know using any of the letters of the alphabet. During reading, they continue to complete missing letters, and after reading, they can complete their entries with help from others, if needed.

MATERIALS:

Paper
Pens/pencils

DIRECTIONS:

Students put their names on their papers and then list the letters of the alphabet on the left side of a piece of paper. Next to each letter, each student writes one self-descriptive word or phrase. Display lists.

If you use this as a game, students do not write their names on the papers. Collect the completed papers, number them, hand them out randomly, and allow students to guess the identities of the authors. The game can continue as long as interest or time warrants.

Example:

A: active
B: belongs to a club
C: can't skate too well
D: dislikes liver
E: enthusiastic
F: fun to be around
G: goes to the library a lot
H: has a pet
I: is a good friend to have

J: just likes a quiet day
K: kinesthetic
L: loves to read
M: makes a good friend
N: nosy
O: orders tacos
P: puts things in order
Q: quick to respond to e-mails
R: reads!

S: scalloping, a favorite sport
T: takes time for family
U: unbiased
V: vehement about education
W: water sports
X: X-ray machine at airports as I travel are a pain
Y: yard work
Z: zooms around

Are You Annoyed?

Something usually sets off a student when he or she acts out. This activity helps you understand, for future reference, what each of your students finds annoying.

ACADEMIC APPLICATION:

Antagonists abound in literature and history. Ask students to create a list of antagonists in literature or history and then describe their annoying characteristics. As a writing activity, each student can then select one characteristic and explain why this behavior is annoying and how the behavior can be avoided or changed.

MATERIALS:

Chart paper for each group
Markers

DIRECTIONS:

Place students in small groups of three or four. Ask them to discuss what annoys them and then list those annoyances on the chart paper. After everyone in the small group has had a chance to contribute to the list, allow time for each group to share their lists with the class.

Prepare a class chart that incorporates student responses for display. At any time during the school year, students can add to this list—as long as the students unanimously agree on the "annoying" statement.

What Annoys Us

1. Boring lessons in school
2. The teacher always talking to us
3. Teachers who don't respect us
4. Homework
5. Not allowed to have iPods in school
6. Kids who disrupt the class
7. Being embarrassed in front of the class
8. Parents always telling me what to do
9. When I lose privileges at home
10. Not having enough time at my locker

Collage of Self

This activity allows students to share information, photos, and illustrations about themselves. Learning new information about others can lead to newfound friendships.

ACADEMIC APPLICATION:

Create a collage for a character in a fiction selection. Categories can include what the character looks like, how the character behaves, what others think of the character, the character's hobbies or interests, the character's friends, and the character's family life. A biographical, non-fiction collage can include real-life information about the character, such as his family life, education, inspirations, or accomplishments.

MATERIALS:

One 9" x 12" sheet of construction paper for each student
A variety of different colored sheets of construction paper
Markers, pens
Computers (if available)

DIRECTIONS:

Each student creates a photo collage from the piece of construction paper, cutting square, rectangle, and oval shapes into the paper. (Students can make their collages larger or smaller if they like.)

Students paste white paper (to write on) underneath each cut-out shape.

Students create a subject title above each shape. Suggested titles include the following:

- Hobbies/interests
- Family
- Likes/dislikes
- Obstacles in life
- Goals in life
- Favorite Things:
  – Movies
  – Video games
  – Music artists
  – Places to shop
  – Books
  – School subjects
  – Restaurants
  – Websites
  – Sports
  – Hangouts

Students then write brief descriptions in each section of the collage. Writing a draft and then typing the information to fit inside the shape makes the collage much more attractive.

Students illustrate the collage with pictures, drawings, photos, stickers, scrapbooking material, etc. Students with computer access can use a search engine to search for images to use as illustrations.

Display collages for all to see. Provide time for students to do a gallery walk to view each other's collages. Ask students to make notes about interesting facts they learned about their peers. Allow time to share what they found interesting.

Getting to Know You

All too often students only get to know others they think are "cool." In this activity, student pairs interview each other and present the information each gathers to the class. Everyone gets to know everyone else. Use one of the partnering techniques suggested in the Introduction, or simply use a count-off system.

ACADEMIC APPLICATION:

In pairs, students write interview questions for a fictional character or non-fictional figure. Once the interview questions are complete, one student takes on the persona of interviewer, and the partner becomes the interviewee. See the Podcasting activity on p. 51.

MATERIALS:

Interview questions
Paper
Pens/pencils

DIRECTIONS:

Create student pairs and distribute the **Interview** handout on p. 6.

Provide time for students to conduct interviews and prepare their written interviews.

Provide time for students to practice their presentations with their partners.

When it's time for students to present their information to the class, copy and distribute the interview questions or show them on a whiteboard or document camera. Each student should get a copy of the **Presentation Critique Form** (p. 7) to complete as he or she listens to each interview. Because students are talking about each other, they must agree on what the person is saying about him. Let students know that eye contact with the audience is important, as is reading fluently.

If possible, videotape the interview presentations; students love watching themselves on camera!

If a computer, document camera, or whiteboard is available, students might want to create a visual presentation that incorporates photos and drawings to accompany their oral-interview reports.

Getting to Know You
THE INTERVIEW

You may select questions from the list below or write other questions of your own. Questions and responses must be written on separate sheets of paper. Once you have completed the interviews, you will prepare your presentation. The information you share does not have to be in the order the questions are listed.

You will turn in your questions and answers along with your presentation. Your presentation must be at least two minutes long, so be sure to practice to see whether you have included enough information. Study the presentation rubric for specific presentation skills for which you should aim.

Interview Questions

1. What are your hobbies and interests?

2. What are your favorite foods?

3. What are your favorite restaurants?

4. What type of music do you listen to, and who are your favorite musicians/groups?

5. What are your favorite TV shows?

6. Where do you usually hang out?

7. How do you feel about school? Explain.

8. What are your favorite subjects? What are your least favorite subjects?

9. What is your favorite book? Explain why.

10. What do you consider to be your strength?

11. What three words might be used to describe yourself? Explain.

12. What is your family life like?

13. What chores are you responsible for doing?

14. Do you have any pets? If so, describe them.

15. What is your job like?

16. Who is the person who influences you most? Explain.

Getting to Know You
PRESENTATION CRITIQUE FORM

Presenter: _____

Person interviewed: _____

	Excellent	Good	Fair	Poor
Presentation flowed smoothly				
Presenter spoke fluently with expression and good rate of speed				
Information was well written and interesting				
Presenter made eye contact with audience				
Evidence of practice				

What could the presenter have done to make the presentation better?

_____

_____

_____

_____

_____

_____

Graffiti Wall

The Latin root of *graffiti* means *to write*. Over time, the word has taken on the negative connotation of defacement of public or private property. Most students have probably seen examples of graffiti on train cars, highway overpasses, and buildings. Graffiti is used in this activity as positive way of getting students to share their thoughts and feelings in a positive, non-threatening way.

⊙ *Teacher Tip*

⠂ *Many classroom-*
⠂ *appropriate images of*
⠂ *graffiti can be found by*
⠂ *doing an Internet search.*

ACADEMIC APPLICATION:

Place academic questions from content-area study on the bricks of the graffiti wall for students to respond to.

MATERIALS:

Large sheet of bulletin board or butcher-block paper divided into segments to resemble bricks
Markers

DIRECTIONS:

Create a brick wall on the bulletin board paper or butcher-block brown paper, and write one question/statement on each brick on the wall.

Instruct students to respond to the question or statement in each brick.

Suggestions for brick statements/topic questions:

- Favorite hangout
- Favorite video game
- Favorite book
- Favorite restaurant
- Favorite website
- Favorite musical group
- Favorite TV show
- Favorite team
- Best friend
- Favorite school subject
- Least favorite school subject
- Favorite after school activity
- Best part of the school day
- Favorite weekend activity

- What sport(s) do you play?
- What sport(s) do you watch?
- Chores you do around your house
- How can we improve the school day?

- How can we improve classroom lessons?
- What irritates you the most?
- What do you do to make yourself feel better when you are upset?

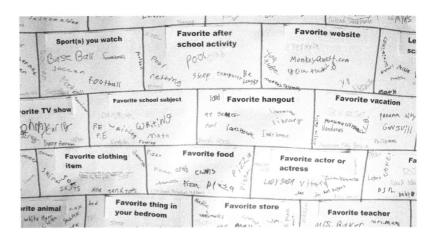

Me Bags or Boxes

This activity is a fun way for students to share information about themselves while practicing speaking, listening, and viewing. A **Presentation Rubric** is on the next page.

ACADEMIC APPLICATION:

Create a bag or box with artifacts representing story elements or use those that represent concepts from a unit of study. Students present to the class, describing each item as it relates to the story or unit of study.

MATERIALS:

Bag or box for each student (students can supply these themselves)
Markers, stickers, materials to decorate bags
Paper
Pens/pencils

Inside each bag or box, students place the following:

- Favorite article of clothing
- Menu from favorite restaurant
- Significant school-related item
- Family photo
- Artifact showing hobby or interest
- Favorite book or magazine
- Artifact showing favorite get-away or vacation spot
- Most prized possession (Students might not want to bring these articles to school, so they may include a representation or bring an illustration instead if they so desire.)

DIRECTIONS:

Provide time in class for students to decorate their boxes or bags. After they are decorated, students take the bags or boxes home to fill with their artifacts. Students write a brief statement or two explaining why each item is significant to them.

Over a one-week period, provide class time each day for several students to present the contents of their bags or boxes.

Me Bags or Boxes
PRESENTATION RUBRIC

Name: _____

_____ Bag/box is decorated attractively; name is evident. . . . . *10 POINTS*

_____ All required material is in the bag/box

    ❏ Favorite article of clothing . . . . *5 POINTS*

    ❏ Menu from favorite restaurant . . . . *5 POINTS*

    ❏ Significant school-related item . . . . *5 POINTS*

    ❏ Family photo. . . . . *5 POINTS*

    ❏ Artifact showing hobby or interest . . . . *5 POINTS*

    ❏ Favorite book or magazine. . . . . *5 POINTS*

    ❏ Artifact showing favorite get-away or vacation spot . . . . *5 POINTS*

    ❏ Most prized possession (item or illustration). . . . . *5 POINTS*

_____ Write up for each item explains its significance

    ❏ Favorite article of clothing . . . . *5 POINTS*

    ❏ Menu from favorite restaurant . . . . *5 POINTS*

    ❏ Significant school-related item . . . . *5 POINTS*

    ❏ Family photo. . . . . *5 POINTS*

    ❏ Artifact showing hobby or interest . . . . *5 POINTS*

    ❏ Favorite book or magazine. . . . . *5 POINTS*

    ❏ Artifact showing favorite get-away or vacation spot . . . . *5 POINTS*

    ❏ Most prized possession (item or illustration). . . . . *5 POINTS*

_____ Presentation: student speaks fluently; makes eye contact
with audience; the audience can easily hear . . . . *10 POINTS*

_____ /100

Personal Website Poster

Students share personal information through a motivating website design created on paper or on a computer.

ACADEMIC APPLICATION:

Create a website on a poster for a fictional or non-fictional reading selection. Fictional categories might include literary elements, setting, plot, characters, conflict/resolution, and theme. For a non-fiction website, instruct students to provide information applicable to a unit of study.

MATERIALS:

Half sheet of poster board per student

Computers, if available

Markers, pens, pencils

Personal photos, pictures, or illustrations

DIRECTIONS:

If you are working with the paper website poster, tell students to set their posters up as collages. One segment will function as the home section on which students list their categories. Beside each category, students place a symbol that corresponds to the symbol on that Web section.

For example, different colored "buttons" can be used to designate each section. A blue button would be placed on the home section next to "All About Me," and a blue button will also be on the "All About Me" section. A red button might be placed on the home section next to "My Family" and a red button will also be placed on the "My Family" section, etc. (See illustration following.)

Students set up their websites on the poster board to include the following categories, or categories of their choice, and color-link the categories with the home section listings. Some suggestions for topics:

- All about me
- My family
- Hobbies and interests
- Likes and dislikes
- My goals
- Miscellaneous facts

Students provide information about each category and write or type the information to be placed on their websites. They paste the home section and their individual Web sections randomly on the poster along with illustrations.

Students title their poster webpage with www.theirname.com.

Teacher Tip

If students create their personal websites on a computer, consider showing a model or two to help them understand what they should include. Most authors have their own websites, which are easy to access and show as models.

Rhetorical Rally

In pairs, students share personal facts about themselves in timed sessions.

ACADEMIC APPLICATION:

After discussing a topic of study for ten minutes or so, provide timed rallies for student pairs to discuss facts about unit concepts with one another. Suggested academic topics to share:

- Discuss the plot in a reading selection
- Discuss the characters in a reading selection
- Discuss a concept in a subject area
- Volley back and forth examples of vocabulary words. For the word ubiquitous, for example, urban students might write McDonald's, Starbucks, Walgreens, CVS, banks, grocery stores, strip malls, cars. Rural students might list cows, fields, feed stores, pick-up trucks, farmers, tractors, barns.

DIRECTIONS:

Write a topic on the board, overhead, or document camera (see suggestions below).

Pair students, and explain that each pair will discuss the topic selected for discussion for a timed period.

One student in each pair begins by responding to the discussion topic. The other student then responds, and the rhetorical rally continues until time is up.

One minute per student is enough time for each partner to share ideas on a given topic. Time can easily be adjusted after the first round if necessary. Search the Web for *free online timer* to find a timer for the rally.

Walk the classroom and listen as students share ideas.

When the timer goes off, students change partners and repeat the process under the same timed conditions. After all students have a chance to share the topic with several students, choose and display a new topic and repeat the process.

Suggested Rapport-building Topics to Discuss:

- What did you do during the summer?
- What did you do during a vacation?
- What are your goals in school?
- Tell about yourself.
- What are you good at doing?
- What are you not so good at doing?
- What do you like about school?
- What don't you like about school?
- What do you do in your free time?
- Tell about your family
- What sports do you play or what teams are you on?
- What would you do if you won a million dollars?

Self Pop-up

In this activity, students use figurative language to describe themselves. A brief mini-lesson about figurative language may be needed.

🔘 *Teacher Tip*

Students love to use this activity to create gifts for special occasion days, such as Mother's Day and Father's Day or birthdays.

Simile: compares two objects using *like* or *as*
The fish was as big as a whale.

Metaphor: compares two things
The fish is a monster.

Alliteration: words that all begin with the same sound
Sally sells seashells by the seashore.

Hyperbole: gross exaggeration
I went fishing and caught a million fish.

Imagery: mental images that appeal to the senses.
The girl's flowing hair cascaded over her shoulders.

The **Figurative Language Scavenger Hunt Mini-book Template** on p. 86 would also be an excellent activity to introduce the Self Pop-up.

ACADEMIC APPLICATION:

Pop-ups are an extremely versatile activity. Students can create pop-ups for concepts or information in any area of study, content-area vocabulary, characters in fiction, or biographies.

MATERIALS:

One 9" x 12" tag board for each student; file folders cut to this size also work well
Construction paper
Photo of self
Markers, pens, pencils

OPTIONAL MATERIALS:

Computers
Scrapbooking material
Stickers

DIRECTIONS:

Students first use an example of figurative language to create a statement or phrase that describes themselves, including an example of simile, metaphor, alliteration, and hyperbole. They also compose a paragraph of three or more sentences that employs imagery. Students label each example of figurative language, preferably by typing the words and cutting them out as labels.

Self Pop-up (continued)

1. Students create their pop-ups by folding the tag board or sized file folders in half from one 9" side to the other.

2. After folding, students create pedestals by cutting two slits approximately 1" long and 1" apart on the fold for placing photos or illustrations in their pop-ups. Students can make several pedestals to attach photos or illustrations depending on the number of items they want on the pop-up, placing slits anywhere along the fold.

3. Students unfold the paper so that it sits in an L-shape on their desks, with the interior of the "L" facing them. They then pop out the cut segment toward themselves and crease it. This becomes the pedestal of the pop-up, onto which their figurative-language descriptions and illustrations are glued.

Display the pop-ups in the classroom, and allow time for students to view them.

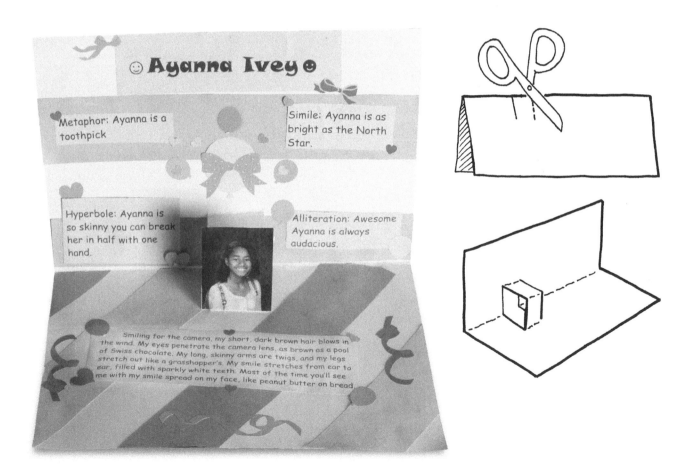

Student Directory

In this activity, each student creates an entry for a student directory. The entries can be compiled electronically or can be cut and pasted to form the directory. Each student receives a copy of the directory. The **Student Data Sheet** is provided to note students' interests and e-mail addresses.

ACADEMIC APPLICATION:

Create a directory of characters taken from a unit of study, such as explorers or scientists or plants or animals or even the periodic table.

MATERIALS:

Computer access to generate directory entries
Paper/pencils

DIRECTIONS:

Model a directory entry, or use the one provided below.

Each student creates his own directory entry along with his e-mail address. It's up to your discretion whether you want to include phone numbers.

Each entry begins with the student's last name and first name followed by a listing of the student's likes and dislikes. Once entries are typed, preferably all in the same typeface and point size, they are compiled to create an alphabetical student directory distributed to each student. For ease of assembly, entries can be cut and pasted to form the directory.

Ideas for Student Entries:

Favorites:

- Video games
- Music group
- Books
- Movies
- Food
- Restaurants
- Places to hang out
- Subjects in school
- Pets
- Vacation spots
- Sports
- Hobbies
- Friends
- Websites

Sample Entry:

Timmons, Candi. Loves rap and hip-hop; reads a lot; favorite place: the library; tacos; hates math; likes to hang with the girls; candiissweet@gmail.com.

Sample Teacher Response:

"Glad to see you like to read; I do, too. I also love tacos. My favorite place to eat is Taco Bell. I prefer pop music over rap, but I do like a few hip-hop artists."

Student Directory
STUDENT DATA SHEET

Name	Hobbies/Interests	Likes	Dislikes	E-mail

Thread Twirl

This activity allows students to talk about themselves. There's a catch, though: their talk lasts as long as the length of their strings! Many students wish their threads were shorter, so beware of surreptitious attempts to cut the thread.

ACADEMIC APPLICATION:

Use the thread twirl to review or discuss concepts in content-area topics or to summarize literary text.

MATERIALS:

Several spools of thread (dental floss works best because it is difficult to tear)

DIRECTIONS:

Pass several spools of thread, string, or dental floss around the classroom, and ask students to each tear or cut off a piece. Let each student take as much or as little thread as he wants.

Tell each student to look at the size of his neighbor's thread. Students cannot cut their thread during the activity and will tell on each other if one tries to make his thread shorter!

Determine the order students will speak so each student knows when his turn will be.

Explain that each student will talk about himself as he winds the thread around his finger. Students with a short piece of thread will not have much time to talk; those who took large pieces must talk for a longer time.

> ### ⦿ *Teacher Tip*
>
> *If this activity is done a second time, most students will take a short piece of thread so they do not have to say much. To prevent this from happening, simply place various sizes of pieces of thread, string, or dental floss in a sealed envelope, and distribute one envelope to each student.*

To Know Me Is to Love Me

This activity gives you a particularly good opportunity to assess students' English-language skills while you are learning about them personally. A **Data-Collection Rubric** is provided on the next page to help you gather the data.

ACADEMIC APPLICATION:

Just about any academic subject lends itself to this format, from vocabulary or literary elements and cause-and-effect practice or math operations.

MATERIALS:

12" x 18" construction paper (one per student)
9" circle on white construction paper (one per student)
Fastener (one per student)
Scissors

◉ *Teacher Tip*

You can diagnose the sentence-writing skills of your students with this activity and use the information to guide and plan your instruction. If students place a text box on the opposite side of the wheel, it becomes a good tool for math problems and answers, vocabulary words and definitions, cause and effect, and much, much more.

DIRECTIONS:

Construct a model of the wheel, and explain how it will be used in this activity. Students write one sentence about themselves in each text box of the wheel. The cover of the wheel is illustrated to depict facts from the students' lives: family, pets, likes, dislikes, hobbies, interests, etc.

1. Give each student one 12" x 18" sheet of construction paper and one 9" circle cut out of another piece of white construction paper.

2. Students fold the construction paper from one 12" side to the other.

3. Students open the folded piece of paper and center the circle on the right half of the sheet of paper. Make sure they leave half an inch of leeway between the centerfold line and the circle. When they fold the paper, they will be able to see a part of the circle extend beyond the right edge. If it is placed on the fold, the circle will not turn.

4. With a pen or pencil, students poke a hole through the center of the circle and the unfolded construction paper underneath it.

5. Students refold the construction paper and flip it over so that the side with the hole poked through it is facing up. They then poke a pen or pencil through this hole again, through the circle in the middle, and out the other side of the construction paper.

6. Students insert a fastener through all three sheets of paper.

7. On one side of the folded paper, students measure 2" down from the top center and cut a box 2 ½" wide and 1 ½" high.

Students then prepare five or six sentences about themselves and write a sentence on each text box. Students can also type their sentences and cut and paste them into the text boxes.

After this activity, display completed wheels for students to see.

Variation:
A text box can be created on the front of the wheel and on the back of the wheel. Sentences on the front of the wheel can be about the student outside of school, and sentences on the reverse side of the wheel can be about the student in school.

To Know Me Is To Love Me
DATA-COLLECTION RUBRIC

This simple rubric allows you to check off the information gathered during this activity to assess how well students can write sentences.

Student's name	Writes fragments	Writes simple sentences	Can vary sentence structure	Needs assistance with punctuation

Academic Applications for the Establishing Rapport Activities

For ease of use, the Academic Applications from the Establishing Rapport Activities have been collected below.

A to Z: All About Me

This activity can be applied to all content areas. Before studying a content topic, students can complete words they know using any of the letters of the alphabet. During reading, they continue to complete missing letters, and after reading, they can help one another complete their entries.

Are You Annoyed?

Antagonists abound in literature and history. Ask students to create a list of antagonists in literature or history and then describe their annoying characteristics. As a writing activity, each student can then select one characteristic, explain why this behavior is annoying, and how the behavior can be avoided or changed.

Collage of Self

Create a collage for a character in a fiction selection. Categories can include what the character looks like, how the character behaves, what others think of the character, the character's hobbies or interests, the character's friends, and the character's family life. A biographical, non-fiction collage can include real-life information about the character, such as his family life, education, inspirations, or accomplishments.

Getting to Know You

In pairs, students write interview questions for a fictional character or non-fictional figure. Once the interview questions are complete, one student takes on the persona of interviewer, and the partner becomes the interviewee. See the Podcasting activity on p. 51.

Graffiti Wall

Place academic questions from the content area being studied on the bricks of the graffiti wall for students to respond to.

Me Bags or Boxes

Create a bag or box with artifacts representing story elements or artifacts representing concepts from a unit of study. Students present to the class, describing each item as it relates to the story or unit of study.

Personal Website Poster

Create a website on a poster for a fictional or non-fictional reading selection. Fictional categories might include literary elements, setting, plot, characters, conflict/resolution, and theme. For a non-fiction website, instruct students to provide information applicable to a unit of study.

Rhetorical Rally

After discussing a topic of study for ten minutes or so, provide time for students to rally concept facts back and forth to review what has been discussed in class.

Self Pop-up

Pop-ups are an extremely versatile activity. Students can create pop-ups for all areas of study: vocabulary in all content areas, concepts, characters in fiction, or people in non-fiction.

Student Directory

Create a directory of characters in a selection or unit of study: explorers, scientists, war heroes, places, elements, plants, or animals.

Thread Twirl

Use the thread twirl to review or discuss concepts content-area topics or to summarize literary text.

To Know Me Is to Love Me

Just about any academic subject lends itself to this format, from vocabulary or literary elements to cause-and-effect practice or math operations.

PART TWO

Engaging Activities That Build Academic Skills

"Education is not the filling of a pail, but the lighting of a fire."

— WILLIAM BUTLER YEATS, POET

Academic Songs or Raps

Students enjoy listening to music. Because music is a powerful motivator, provide an opportunity for students to turn their literature selections or any other content material into a rap or song lyrics. In this activity, students incorporate the literary elements of plot, setting, and characters into a song or rap.

MATERIALS:

Paper/pencils
Content-area material: notes, texts

DIRECTIONS:

Before presenting this lesson, present a mini-lesson during which students listen to a song and follow along with the lyrics.

Once students have listened to the song, divide them into small groups. Instruct each group to analyze the song lyrics and look for the main idea of each stanza.

Allow the small groups to discuss the lyrics. Talk about the message the author wants to communicate, rhythm/rhyme pattern, and any literary elements or figurative language.

Students now use their subject-area material as a basis for writing their own songs or raps. If they are writing a song or rap for a novel, students can be divided into small groups with each group assigned a chapter of the selection.

Students share their completed songs or raps with the class. If this activity is done throughout several days, they can choose to come to class in costume.

This activity is fun to videotape. Students get a kick out of watching themselves. If your school has an in-school TV show, segments can be played for all students to view.

Song composed from *Holes* by Louis Sachar: (Sung to the tune of "I Will Survive" by Gloria Gaynor)

At first she was afraid
She was petrified
Kept thinking she would never live without Sam by her side
But then she thought so many nights about how Sam was amiss
And now she's killin' every man
'N sealing it with a kiss.

And then you came
To get the loot,
But I said no way,
And I gave you the ol' boot.

Rap composed from *The Pearl* by John Steinbeck

"The Song of the Family"

This is the story all about how
Kino's family stuck together
No matter how

Treating each other
With the utmost of care
But the pearls tempted them
They were always there

In a little village
Kino's family hung
Scorpion came down
And Coyotito was stung

It seemed like all of their hope was lost
Doctor wouldn't treat him
They couldn't pay the cost
But they didn't give up hope
They turned to the sea
To make some cash for the family

Their pearling plan did unfurl
And Kino found the pearl of the world

Doctor came by
Now Coyotito will be OK
For them it had been a wonderful day

News spread around that the family was rich
But into the sea the pearl Kino would pitch.

Active Concept Review

This activity gives students the opportunity to work at their own paces and to move around the room as they review content-area concepts and topics.

This non-threatening activity keeps students moving during a lesson review. Students are only required to answer questions they know the answers to, and it allows them to ask questions about what they are unable to answer.

◉ *Teacher Tip*

- *For a civics or American*
- *government review, the United*
- *States government has an*
- *excellent website with 100*
- *questions used in the U.S.*
- *citizen naturalization test. You*
- *can find these questions at*
- **www.uscis.gov/newtest**.

MATERIALS:

Academic questions from a unit of study
Answer key
One sheet of notebook paper per student
Pens/pencils

DIRECTIONS:

For this activity, the teacher or the students can create the questions. If the teacher creates the questions, she writes one question for each student. If the students create the questions, read them first and select which ones to use. If you run short on questions, create some yourself.

Number the questions and create an answer key, matching answers to the corresponding question number.

To begin the activity, students number a sheet of notebook paper from one to the last question number. Randomly distribute one numbered question to each student. Instruct students to read the numbered questions they received and answer them next to the corresponding numbers on their papers. For example, if a student receives question seven, he answers it next to the number seven on his numbered paper.

After each student answers his question, he then trades with other students who need another question to answer. Allow adequate time for students to answer all questions.

Once students have answered the questions, place your answer key in a central location, and allow students to check their answers. You can randomly place several answer keys around the classroom for students to gather and check their answers, or you can place the answers on the document camera or board. During this activity, you will be available to answer questions for students who incorrectly answer any questions.

Once all students have completed all questions and checked their answers, hold a class discussion to talk about questions with which students had difficulty.

Questions from this activity can be used when it's time to assess the material from which the questions were created.

And the Winner Is . . .

This activity is presented in the form of an awards show with the teacher acting as the show's host. Each student writes two speeches: one in the first person to read when accepting the award, and one in the third person that the host reads as she introduces the award winner. Each student creates an award that the host will present to him or her.

◉ *Teacher Tip*

- *Everyone wants fifteen*
- *minutes of fame. You get*
- *yours by hosting the show.*
- *The students get theirs when*
- *they receive their awards.*

Students get good practice writing a speech in the first- and third-person viewpoints. Presenting to a group encourages active listening skills. It also encourages students to practice their public-speaking skills in front of an audience.

MATERIALS:

Reading material

Paper/pencils

Craft material (wood pieces, Styrofoam, stickers, Popsicle® sticks, scrapbooking material, construction paper, empty paper towel and toilet paper holders, pipe cleaners, empty cans, etc.)

DIRECTIONS:

Distribute and discuss the **Grading Rubric** requirements (see p. 29). Review the **And the Winner Is . . . Example** on p. 30.

After reading a biography, a novel, or completing a unit of study involving people, instruct students to select a person to whom they will present an award.

Provide class time for students to research the person they selected to win an award.

After researching their award winner, each student:

- writes one speech in the third person that functions as an introduction for this person before he accepts his award.
- writes one speech in the first person that thanks everyone who inspired him or selected him for this award and to what he credits his success.
- designs an award for presentation.

Students must include the following information:

First-person Speech

- Thanks everyone who nominated him
- Tells who or what inspired this person
- Tells to whom or what he credits his success

Third-person Speech

- Highlights this person's accomplishments
- Tells how this person rose to fame
- Does not mention the person's name until the last sentence

And the Winner Is . . . (continued)

With speeches written and awards created, the show begins. The TV show host reads the third-person introductory speech, and the person accepts his award using the first-person speech. This activity is fun to record and watch again later.

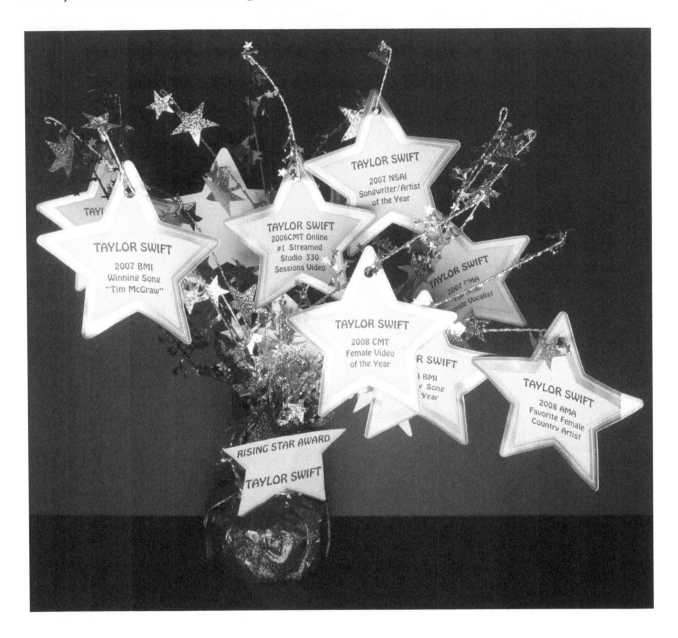

And the Winner Is . . .
GRADING RUBRIC

Name: _____

_____ Third person speech highlights the person's accomplishments; tells how this
person rose to fame; only mentions award winner's name in the last sentence . . . *10 POINTS*

_____ First-person speech thanks everyone who nominated this person for this
award; tells who or what inspired you and to what you credit your success . . . . *10 POINTS*

_____ Speeches are written using correct grammar, punctuation, spelling,
varied sentence structure, and complete sentences. . . . . *10 POINTS*

_____ Award includes the person's name and accomplishments; reflects the
award being given; neat/attractive presentation; creative presentation . . . . *10 POINTS*

_____ Evidence that the speech was well rehearsed; plenty of eye contact
with audience. . . . . *5 POINTS*

_____ Signature on speeches indicates a parent/guardian listened to you
practice your speech . . . . *5 POINTS*

_____ /50   *FINAL GRADE*

And the Winner Is . . .
EXAMPLE

And the Winner is . . . Taylor Swift

THIRD-PERSON, INTRODUCTORY SPEECH:

From growing up on a Christmas tree farm in Wyomissing, Pennsylvania, to spending most of her time on tour buses traveling across the country, our next award winner burst onto the scene at the age of 16 with a debut single about another country music artist, Tim McGraw. It ran up the charts all the way to #6. That was the first of five singles from her self-titled debut album, which is a triple platinum album. She is the first female solo artist in country-music history to write or co-write every song on a platinum-selling debut album. She writes, sings, plays guitar and piano, and entertains audiences with her life stories put to music about true events that happened during her high-school years.

Her self-titled debut album sold more than 5 million copies. In October 2007, she was the youngest artist to win the Songwriter/Artist of the Year award from the Nashville Songwriters Association, an award on which other songwriters voted.

In November 2007, this artist won the CMA's Horizon Award, and in 2008 she won the Academy of Country Music's Top New Female Vocalist award. In 2009, this singer won the MTV's Video Music Awards for Best Female Video. I am proud to present the Rising Star Award to Taylor Swift.

FIRST-PERSON SPEECH (to be read by the student doing the project):

Wow! I love my music, but I must say that my fans are the best. I love you! I showed you all how much I love you when I won CMT's Breakthrough Video of the Year award and let all my fans pose with my award. I want all my fans to know that I, too, am your fan.

I want to thank my parents who upped and moved to Tennessee just for my music career. They really believed in me. And I can't forget Scott Borchetta who had faith in me and signed me to Big Machine Records. I hope to keep touring, and hopefully you all can see me in your hometowns. And I finally want to thank all of my old boyfriends and crushes who inspired me to write most of my songs. Again, thanks and I love you!

Character Connections

In this activity, students make personal connections to the characters, the setting, and the conflict from a reading selection.

MATERIALS:

One sheet of construction paper of any size for each student
Pens, pencils

DIRECTIONS:

1. Provide each student with one sheet of paper. Students fold the paper so that the two longer sides meet (hotdog fold).

2. Students then cut three slits on the top section of the paper, each an equal distance apart from the bottom of the paper to the fold .

3. Students label the top sections as follows:
   Section one: characters in the selection
   Section two: setting(s) of the selection
   Section three: conflicts in the selection

4. Under each corresponding flap, students write the following connections:
   personal connections to the characters
   personal connections to the setting
   personal connections to the conflicts

Provide time for students to share their responses. Display students' work.

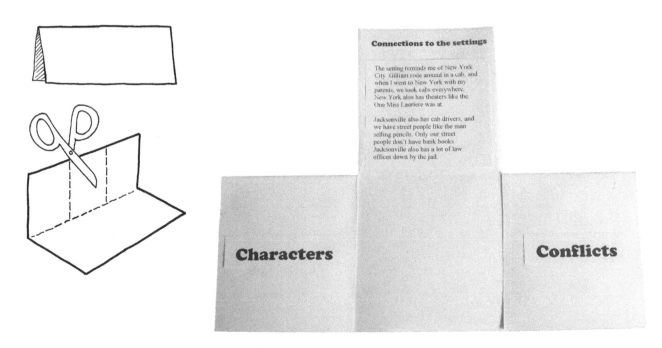

Chunking the Text

This activity allows students to focus on one section of text at a time for practice with close and critical reading. Depending upon each student's abilities, the chunk of text can be as small as several sentences or a paragraph or as long as a chapter.

Struggling readers, or those reading difficult text, often benefit from dividing the text into smaller chunks.

MATERIALS:

Text being studied
Graphic organizer (below)
Pens/pencils

DIRECTIONS:

Break the text to be read into manageable chunks. You can differentiate instruction here by chunking the text in different places for students of different abilities. Each different assignment can be copied on different colored paper so students will know who is working on the same chunks of text. You might want to allow students to sit by others who are reading the same chunk of text.

Review the **Graphic Organizer Example** on p. 34. Each student will need his or her prepared text with one graphic organizer for each chunk of text. Graphic organizers can be copied with several on one page (see the template on p. 33).

As students read the first assigned chunk of text, they stop to complete the following on their graphic organizer: write any questions, note unfamiliar words, make connections, and provide a brief summary.

After students have completed reading a chunk of text and have completed their graphic organizers, allow them to collaborate with others who have read the same chunk of text to discuss the information on their graphic organizers.

Students then move on to their next chunk of text and repeat the process until all assigned chunks have been read. As a class, students can then discuss the selection, with the teacher facilitating the discussion.

Teacher Tip

- *Chunking the text*
- *makes differentiated*
- *instruction easy!*

Chunking the Text
GRAPHIC ORGANIZER

Reading Selection: _____

Chunk of text read (page(s)):
Questions I have:
Words I don't know:
Connections I can make:
Summary of text:

Chunking the Text
GRAPHIC ORGANIZER EXAMPLE

Reading Selection: _"The King of Mazy May"_

Chunk of text read (page(s)): Paragraph four
Questions I have: What did they discover? What kind of strange things happened to the men who worked upon the creek?
Words I don't know: Yukon Ramparts Mazy May Creek Klondike country toil
Connections I can make: I don't live with my mom, either. My family has hardships, too.
Summary of text: Walt and his dad travel really far probably by walking. They live by the Mazy May River and are working hard and having a lot of problems. Things got good for them, and they were rewarded for their hard work, but strangers are coming and they cause problems.

Cognitive Levels Flip Book

This flip book can be used to challenge students to work at higher cognitive levels. As they create and answer questions at higher cognitive levels, students learn that responses may not be right or wrong but require thinking and rationalizing to get to an answer. Students enjoy thinking outside the box, and they will rise to this challenge.

Before using this activity, you will want to know at which cognitive levels your students are working. To do this, you will assess students on the text being read and complete the data collection chart (see following page).

With so many assessment tools available, it's not difficult to create a cognitive levels data-collection chart as shown. Two data-collection charts are provided; one is based on Bloom's Taxonomy and the other is based on Webb's Depth of Knowledge.

To assess students after reading a selection or unit of study, you can create questions at each cognitive level using either Bloom's Taxonomy or Webb's Depth of Knowledge. Preceding or following each question, note the cognitive level the question represents, such as remembering or evaluating for Bloom's or Level 1 or Level 2 for Webb's. This makes for easy data collection.

Once you grade the assessment, check the boxes corresponding to the cognitive levels in which the students need assistance.

You can use the charts as a guide when assigning question stems for the Cognitive Levels Flip Book. This might seem to be a lot of work, but it really ends up making your work a lot easier. Once you know at which cognitive levels your students are operating, providing differentiated instruction to meet their needs and scaffolding their progress to higher cognitive levels becomes much easier. This is an excellent way to differentiate instruction.

MATERIALS

Two or three sheets of 8 ½" x 11" paper
Pens or pencils
Reading material

DIRECTIONS:

Provide each student with three sheets of 8 ½ x 11" paper. Model how to stagger and stack them approximately half an inch apart.

With the staggered sections facing you, fold the papers away from you so you will now have a flip book of six staggered sections.

Explain that each student will respond to one question at each cognitive level of either Bloom's Taxonomy or Webb's Depth of Knowledge.

Cognitive Levels Flip Book (continued)

If you are using Bloom's Taxonomy, ask students to label each flap of their flip books as follows: *remember, understand, apply, analyze, evaluate,* and *create. Create* goes on the back of the flip book. Have students label the top flap of their flip book, "The Three Little Pigs".

If you are using Webb's Depth of Knowledge, students will label each flap of their flip books as follows: *recall, basic application of skill/concept, strategic thinking,* and *extended thinking.* In the one blank section of this flip book, students can make personal connections to the selection.

Read the story.

If using Bloom's Taxonomy, instruct students to lift the title flap and answer the *remember* question. (They write the *remember* question under the title flap.) They lift the *remember* flap to write the *understand* question and its answer, etc. The questions for each of Bloom's verbs are as follows:

Remember.....Describe the three houses the three little pigs built.

Understand....Summarize the story.

Apply..........Construct a theory as to why each pig built a separate house.

Analyze.........Compare/contrast the Big Bad Wolf's methods of trickery to the little pigs' method of trickery.

Evaluate........Provide an argument to support the Big Bad Wolf's desire to eat the three little pigs.

Create ....Compose an obituary for the Big Bad Wolf.

If using Webb's Depth of Knowledge, instruct students to leave the bottom flap blank. (The blank flap will be used to make personal connections to the selection.) Ask students to lift each of the other flaps, write the following questions under the appropriate flap, and then answer the following questions:

Level 1..........Recall: Describe the three little pigs' houses.

Level 2..........Basic Application of Skill/Concept: Construct a theory as to why each pig built a separate house.

Level 3..........Strategic Thinking: Compare/contrast the Big Bad Wolf's methods of trickery with the little pigs' method of trickery.

Level 4..........Extended Thinking: Compose an obituary for the Big Bad Wolf.

Allow students to share and discuss their responses when the flip books are completed.

 **Teacher Tip**

To make it easy to assign like-leveled students to share their flip books, simply use a different color paper for questions at each cognitive level.

After modeling the different cognitive levels with *The Three Little Pigs*, assign a reading selection or chapter from a unit of study, and instruct students to write one question from each cognitive level using Bloom's Taxonomy or Webb's Depth of Knowledge from the charts on the following page. This helps familiarize the students with the tasks at each cognitive level. Or, you can use the data on your data charts to determine at which level each student is to write his own questions.

Supply each student with a copy of the **Bloom's Taxonomy Verbs** (see p. 41) or **Webb's Depth of Knowledge Chart** (see p. 40) on which you have highlighted the cognitive level(s) at which each student will work.

On the top flap of the cognitive levels flip book, the students write the title of the reading selection or unit title.

On each of the other five flaps, students will write tasks from Bloom's or Webb's, using words from that level of the charts to begin his questions. Instruct students to follow the instructions for the flip book they made for *The Three Little Pigs* activity.

Cognitive Levels Flip Book (continued)

You might want students to write one question from each cognitive level, or you might want to use what you know about your students to assign them one or several cognitive levels from which to write questions.

Once the students have completed writing all five questions, they create an answer key. They then trade their flip books with another student. If all students are writing questions at all cognitive levels, students can trade randomly; if students are assigned various cognitive levels, the teacher must tell the students with whom to trade flip books.

Students answer each other's questions, then return the flip books to their creators, who checks the answers for accuracy.

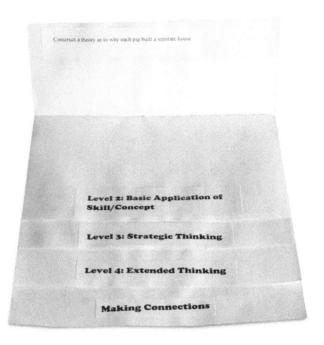

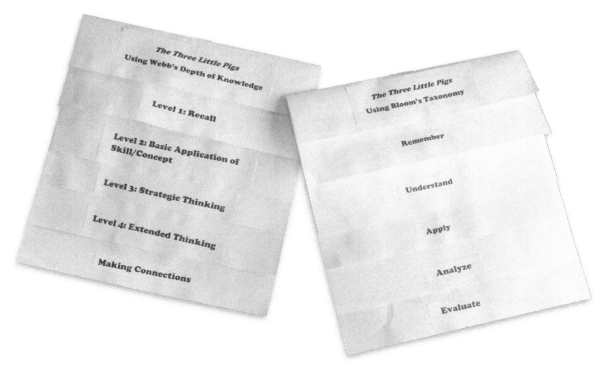

Bloom's Taxonomy
DATA-COLLECTION CHART

Student's name	Remembering	Understanding	Applying	Analyzing	Evaluating	Creating

Webb's Depth of Knowledge Chart
DATA-COLLECTION CHART

Student's name	Level 1: Recall	Level 2: Skill/Concept	Level 3: Strategic Thinking	Level 4: Extended Thinking

Bloom's Taxonomy Verbs

Remembering: Can the student recall or remember the information?	define, duplicate, list, memorize, recall, repeat, reproduce state
Understanding: Can the student explain ideas or concepts?	classify, describe, discuss, explain, identify, locate, recognize, report, select, translate, paraphrase
Applying: Can the student use the information in a new way?	choose, demonstrate, dramatize, employ, illustrate, interpret, operate, schedule, sketch, solve, use, write
Analyzing: Can the student distinguish between the different parts?	appraise, compare, contrast, criticize, differentiate, discriminate, distinguish, examine, experiment, question, test
Evaluating: Can the student justify a stand or decision?	appraise, argue, defend, judge, select, support, value, evaluate
Creating: Can the student create a new product or point of view?	assemble, construct, create, design, develop, formulate, write

Cognitive Levels Flip Book

HESS' COGNITIVE RIGOR MATRIX WITH CURRICULAR EXAMPLES

Bloom's Revised Taxonomy of Cognitive Process Dimensions	Webb's Depth-of-Knowledge (DOK) Levels			
	LEVEL 1 Recall & Reproduction	**LEVEL 2** Skills & Concepts	**LEVEL 3** Strategic Thinking / Reasoning	**LEVEL 4** Extended Thinking
Remember Retrieve knowledge from long-term memory, recognize, recall, locate, identify	Recall, recognize, or locate basic facts, ideas, principles Recall or identify conversions between representations, numbers, or units of measure Identify facts/details in texts			
Understand Construct meaning, clarify, paraphrase, represent, translate, illustrate, give examples, classify, categorize, summarize, generalize, infer a logical conclusion (such as from examples given), predict, compare/contrast, match like ideas, explain, construct models	Compose and decompose numbers Evaluate an expression Locate points (grid, number line) Represent math relationships in words, pictures, or symbols Write sample sentences Select appropriate word for intended meaning Describe/explain how or why	Specify and explain relationships Give non-examples/examples Make and record observations Take notes; organize ideas/data Summarize results, concepts, ideas Make basic inferences or logical predictions from data or texts Identify main ideas or accurate generalizations	Explain, generalize, or connect ideas using supporting evidence Explain thinking when more than one response is possible Explain phenomena in terms of concepts Write full composition to meet specific purpose Identify themes	Explain how concepts or ideas specifically relate to other content domains or concepts Develop generalizations of the results obtained or strategies used and apply them to new problem situations
Apply Carry out or use a procedure in a given situation; carry out (apply to a familiar task), or use (apply) to an unfamiliar task	Follow simple/routine procedure (recipe-type directions) Solve a one-step problem Calculate, measure, apply a rule Apply an algorithm or formula (area, perimeter, etc.) Represent in words or diagrams a concept or relationship Apply rules or use resources to edit spelling, grammar, punctuation, conventions	Select a procedure according to task needed and perform it Solve routine problem applying multiple concepts or decision points Retrieve information from a table, graph, or figure and use it to solve a problem requiring multiple steps Use models to represent concepts Write paragraph using appropriate organization, text structure, and signal words	Use concepts to solve non-routine problems Design investigation for a specific purpose or research question Conduct a designed investigation Apply concepts to solve non-routine problems Use reasoning, planning, and evidence Revise final draft for meaning or progression of ideas	Select or devise an approach among many alternatives to solve a novel problem Conduct a project that specifies a problem, identifies solution paths, solves the problem, and reports results Illustrate how multiple themes (historical, geographic, social) may be interrelated
Analyze Break into constituent parts, determine how parts relate, differentiate between relevant-irrelevant, distinguish, focus, select, organize, outline, find coherence, deconstruct (e.g., for bias or point of view)	Retrieve information from a table or graph to answer a question Identify or locate specific information contained in maps, charts, tables, graphs, or diagrams	Categorize, classify materials Compare/contrast figures or data Select appropriate display data Organize or interpret (simple) data Extend a pattern Identify use of literary devices Identify text structure of paragraph Distinguish relevant - irrelevant information; fact - opinion	Compare information within or across data sets or texts Analyze and draw conclusions from more complex data Generalize a pattern Organize/interpret date; complex graph Analyze author's craft, viewpoint, or potential bias	Analyze multiple sources of evidence or multiple works by the same author, or across genres, or time periods Analyze complex/abstract themes Gather, analyze, and organize information Analyze discourse styles
Evaluate Make judgments based on criteria, check, detect inconsistencies or fallacies, judge, critique			Cite evidence and develop a logical argument for concepts Describe, compare, and contrast solution methods Verify reasonableness of results Justify conclusions made	Gather, analyze & evaluate relevancy & accuracy Draw & justify conclusions Apply understanding in a novel way, provide argument or justification for the application
Create Reorganize elements into new patterns/structures, generate, hypothesize, design, plan, construct, produce	Brainstorm ideas, concepts, or perspectives related to a topic or concept	Generate conjectures or hypotheses based on observations or prior knowledge	Synthesize information within one source or text Formulate an original problem given a situation Develop a complex model for a given situation	Synthesize information across multiple sources or texts Design a model to inform and solve a real-world, complex, or abstract situation

2009 © Hess, Carlock, Jones, & Walkup.

Create a Character

Students will create a graphic organizer to visually represent characters from a fictional selection read.

Readers visualize fictional characters by the way they look, how they behave, and what others think of them. Recognizing physical appearance is a low cognitive-level operation, but for students to use details from the selection to determine a character's behavior and how others perceive the character often requires synthesizing information, a higher cognitive-level skill.

MATERIALS:
One piece of construction paper for each student, 12" x 18" preferred

DIRECTIONS:
1. Fold the paper in half from left to right with the two shorter sides meeting.

2. Fold the paper into three sections from top to bottom.

3. Make three cuts down the folds through the top half of the paper.

4. Students label each section as follows on the top section of the paper:

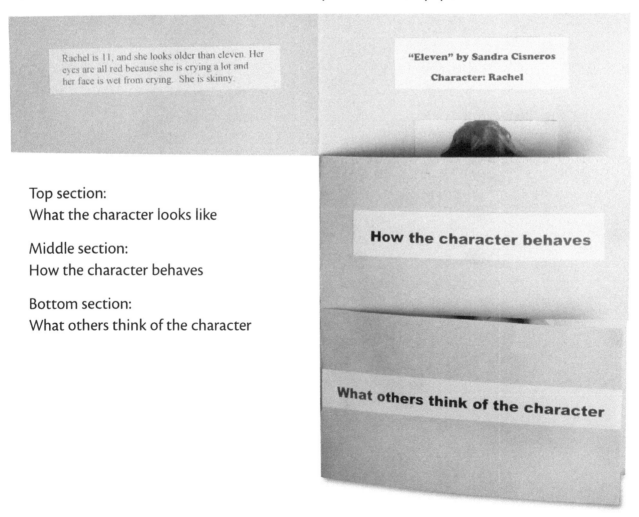

Top section:
What the character looks like

Middle section:
How the character behaves

Bottom section:
What others think of the character

Create a Character (continued)

The order of the tasks for this activity scaffolds information from low to higher cognitive levels, moving from the recall level of Webb's Depth of Knowledge or the Remember Level of Bloom's taxonomy through the middle level of each to find context clues to Level Three of Webb's and Bloom's analysis level. This activity provides an excellent opportunity for teachers to scaffold information and provide a range of complexity.

Students open each section and write descriptions on the reverse side of the labeled section. They must support their response from the text. When describing how the character behaves, students provide examples from the text that indicate how the character behaves. They can include examples of what he does and how he treats others. Students will need to infer what other characters in the selection think about their character through their reactions to him.

Students illustrate a likeness of the character on the side opposite the written descriptions. They can draw an illustration of the character or look through magazines to find a picture of a person who resembles what they believe the character looks like. They can even mix and match images or add accessories and different clothing to make the character appear as they visualize him.

Create a Symbol

After reading a fiction selection, students create a symbol that represents a character.

Symbolism is an abstract concept, and this activity gives students practice with internalizing what they are reading.

MATERIALS:

Fiction reading selection
Paper
Pencils
Items that students deem necessary to create a symbol

DIRECTIONS:

After reading a short story or novel, ask students to think of a symbol that would represent a character in a selection. This symbol will be in the form of a tangible item. For example, a chess board might represent Bella's emotions in the novel *Twilight* by Stephenie Meyer because of Bella's uncertainty about her emotions for Edward and Jacob. Bella is not sure which move to make and how the outcome of any move will affect her.

Allow students time to discuss the selection and time to create their symbols. Written descriptions must include supporting details for their choice of symbol and explain its relevance to the selection.

Allow time for students to share their completed written rationales, and display them in the classroom. Students can bring in examples of the symbols or create illustrations of them as part of the written piece. This creative response to literature can be assessed easily.

⊙ *Teacher Tip*

With extended thinking, students move beyond basic recall to higher cognitive skills. It provides the opportunity for students to demonstrate their critical-thinking abilities, to analyze and synthesize information, and to express their own views that go beyond right and wrong answers. When using Webb's Depth of Knowledge, extended thinking is the highest level of thinking, Level 4. Extended thinking opens the door to excellent classroom discussions.

Create a Symbol (continued)

Some other examples:

Number the Stars by Lois Lowry

- Symbol: a tree

- "I chose a tree to represent Annemarie Johansen because like a tree, as Annemarie ages, she gets bolder and braver. No matter what challenges she faces, she stays strong through it all. Furthermore, she may shed her leaves, but they will always grow back in the end."

Eclipse by Stephenie Meyer

- Symbol: a magnet

- "I compare Bella to a magnet. A magnet attracts metal, and Bella attracts trouble. Also, Bella is attracted to both Edward and Jacob. Finally, magnetic poles are in the center of the Earth, and Bella is the center of Edward's world."

Everlost by Neal Shusterman

- Symbol: a tree branch

- "A tree branch represents Lief. It is where he lives: the treetops. Though it may be hard to break, it is still fragile like his emotions. Yet it can still support life, just as Lief helps the lives of those stuck in *Everlost*."

Give One/Get One Flip Book

This versatile activity is an interactive way for students to sharpen note-taking skills in any academic subject. Students focus on one chunked section of text at a time as they prepare notes for their own flip books. Then they share notes with fellow classmates as they give ideas and get ideas.

MATERIALS:

Two of three sheets of 8 ½" x 11" paper
Pens/pencils
Reading material for note taking

DIRECTIONS:

To prepare the flip book, take three sheets of paper and stagger them approximately half an inch apart. This will create a flip book with six sections. Two sheets can be used for a flip book with four sections. The number of sections you need depends upon the amount of text being read.

Next, with the staggered sections facing you, fold the papers away from you so you have a flip book of six (or four) equally staggered sections. For illustrations that explain how to make the flip books, see the Cognitive Levels Flip Book activity on p. 35.

After creating the flip book, students should fold it in half from the left side to the right so that the long sides meet.

Students write the title of the selection or unit of study on the top flap in the center. Each consecutive flap will be labeled in the center with a specific title for a chunk of text to be read.

A four-section science section flip book might be labeled:

- Atoms (title)
- Protons
- Neutrons
- Electrons

A six-section flip book might chunk difficult text by paragraphs:

- Title of selection
- Paragraphs 1–3
- Paragraphs 4–6
- Paragraphs 7–9
- Paragraphs 10–12
- Paragraphs 13–15

A four-section reading selection might be chunked by page numbers:

- Title of selection
- pp. 244–245
- pp. 246–247
- pp. 248–250

Give One/Get One Flip Book (continued)

Students read the first chunk of text and take notes of important details on the left side of their flip book above the flap that corresponds to the chunk of text. This is the "Give One" column. After a designated amount of time (five minutes is a good place to start), allow students to share what they wrote with their classmates.

The give one/get one of the activity begins here. One student reads his notes to another student. If the listener's notes contain the same details/information for the text chunk, that fact is checked off. If the listener does not have the details/information on his own paper, he writes it down on the right side of the flip book in the "Get One" column. Then the listening partner reads new ideas from his own "Give One" column, if any, for his partner to note in his "Get One" column.

Students now find other partners to repeat the process two or three times, then move to complete the next chunk of text and repeat the give one/get one process.

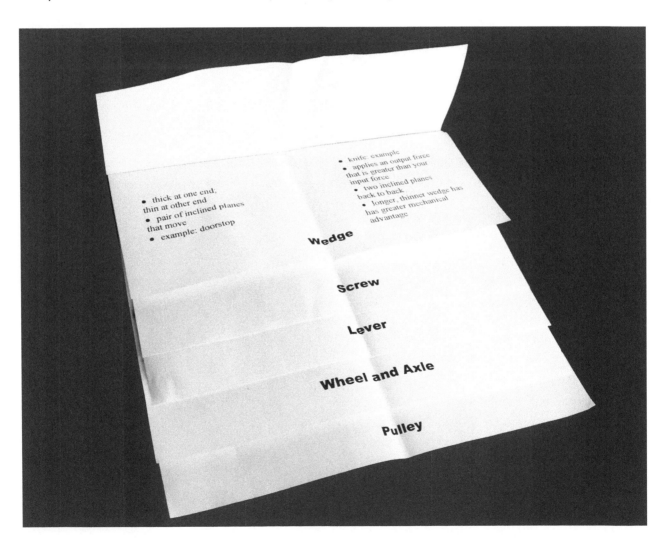

Interactive Bookmark

Before-, during-, and after-reading activities engage students with text. As students read a novel, their interactive bookmarks guide them to look for specific literary elements and standards that will be discussed later in class. Please see the **Interactive Bookmark Example** on p. 50.

This handy reference helps students focus on the questions and concepts that will be assessed. This activity can be used for any length of text, from chunks or chapters to full novels. Knowing in advance what to look for when reading makes for better class discussions and provides a purpose for reading.

MATERIALS:

Novel or reading selection
One interactive bookmark for each student

DIRECTIONS:

Before reading a selection or a novel, prepare a bookmark with the following information:

- Dates the reading assignment will be discussed in class
- A chunk of text to be read by the assigned date; the reading can be chunked by chapters or by pages
- Questions to answer or activities to complete before the assigned reading date

Prepare the bookmark to fit two on one 8 ½" x 11" piece of paper. Distribute one bookmark to each student.

Explain to the students that this bookmark provides them all the assignments for a given period of time. They must complete each assignment by the date given. For those students who want to read ahead and complete assignments in advance, they can do so.

On the date the reading will be discussed, ask the students to take out their assignment due that day. Walk around the room, and note which students completed the assignment. This can be placed in the grade book. Conclude class with a discussion of the assignment.

Interactive Bookmark
EXAMPLE

Freak the Mighty by Rodman Philbrick

Before reading: Respond to #1 and #2
1. What does the title tell you about the book?
2. Describe the characteristics of a true friend.

During reading: Select either the journal activity or chapter title activity for each chapter read, 1 through 25.

- **Journal:** For each chapter read, respond in a journal entry from either Max or Kevin's perspective.
- **Chapter titles:** Each chapter has an interesting title; explain what each chapter's title means using details from the story.

The journal and chapter titles assignment will be checked on the dates listed.

Additional questions during reading assignments:

January 9: chapters 1 – 5
- Describe Max
- Describe Kevin
- Locate one example of figurative language, metaphor, simile, personification, or hyperbole); note the page it is on and be ready to discuss

January 11: chapters 6 – 9
- Create a Venn diagram to compare Blade and his gang with Max and Kevin.
- Why did Blade and his gang decide to pick on Max and Kevin?
- Explain the name "Freak the Mighty." Tell how Max and Kevin got this name.

January 13: chapters 10 – 12
- Select Max or Kevin; describe how this character has changed since the story began. Explain what has caused these changes.

January 16: chapters 13 – 16
- List two conflicts from these chapters. If the conflict was resolved in these chapters, tell how it was resolved.

January 19: chapters 17 – 20
- Create two columns on your paper. Label one *cause*; label the other *effect*. Provide one cause and effect statement from each chapter.

January 24: chapters 21 – 25
- Describe the main conflict in this story. Tell how it was resolved.
- What did Max learn from Kevin?

Post reading: Select one – due January 27
- ➢ Create a timeline of important events in the story.
- ➢ Write a newspaper article about one of Max and Kevin's adventures.
- ➢ Extend the story by writing a conversation Max might have with Kevin once the story ended.

Podcasting

Working in pairs or small groups, students create an audio recording conversation that can be transferred to an iPod or MP3 player.

Technology engages our students. Why not use it to motivate? And what better way to improve a student's fluency than by allowing a student to listen to himself and have others provide feedback?

MATERIALS:

Reading material
Paper
Pencils
Computer
Microphone (Note: Most new computers have built-in microphones)
Free recording and editing software, such as Audacity (**www.audacity.com**)

DIRECTIONS:

To follow up on a reading selection or to extend a unit of study, ask students to choose characters/famous people and create a conversation related to the literary selection or the unit of study. Students should include the following information in their podcasts:

- A brief narrative introducing the topic that provides the rationale for selecting this topic
- Tell what/who inspired this person (character)
- Describe the person's (character's) accomplishments
- Tell how this person (character) had an impact on society
- Provide other interesting information about this person (character)

Each student should compose five questions for their listeners to answer on the **Podcasting Critiquing Rubric** on p. 54. Students can collaborate as they write their own parts of the podcast conversation. A formal **Podcasting Grading Rubric** is available on p. 53.

Students record their podcasts on the computer.

- Open Audacity.
- Hover over the icons to see what each one does.
- Click on the *record* button to record the podcast.
- Once done recording, click on the *back* button to return to the beginning of the podcast.
- To listen to the podcast, click on the *play* button.

Once all podcasts have been recorded, each student downloads someone else's podcast on an iPod or MP3 player. (The students know how to do this.)

After listening, each student listener completes a critique sheet.

Podcasting (continued)

Some suggestions for conversations:

- Two characters from a story discussing a problem or concern
- One scientist to another on the verge of a breakthrough
- A military leader talking to his troops
- Dr. Phil or Oprah giving advice to a fictional character or a famous person
- An interview between a reporter and a famous person or fictional characters

Teacher Tip

*Still not sure where to begin? Visit PoducateMe.com (**www.poducateme.com/ guide**) for a free, step-by-step guide to podcasting. For an overview of the newest version of Audacity, visit **manual.audacityteam. org** and click through the "Tutorials" section. If you'd like to see some examples of podcasts created by (and for) educators, visit the Education Podcast Network: **www.epnweb.org**.*

Podcasting
GRADING RUBRIC

Name: _____

_____ Podcast contains a brief narrative introduction introducing your topic and why you
selected this topic to research. . . . . *5 POINTS*

_____ Podcast includes the following information: (20 points/5 points each)

     ❑ Tell who/what inspired this person (character). . . . . *5 POINTS*

     ❑ Describe this person's (character's) accomplishments . . . . *5 POINTS*

     ❑ How has this person (character) had an affect on society? . . . . *5 POINTS*

     ❑ Other interesting facts about this person . . . . *5 POINTS*

_____ Five questions are available for others to answer after listening to your podcast . . . *5 POINTS*

_____ Written report uses correct grammar, sentence structure, punctuation,
and capitalization . . . . *10 POINTS*

_____ Podcast flows with evidence of practice; sound is audible; minimum
recording time is two minutes . . . . *10 POINTS*

_____ FINAL GRADE/50

Podcasting
CRITIQUING RUBRIC

Evaluator: _____ Date: _____

Name/Title of podcast: _____

What to look for in podcast	Excellent	Good	Fair	Poor
The podcast held my interest.				
The podcast flowed well; it was organized.				
The speakers spoke clearly and were easy to understand.				
Overall, the podcast was…				

Complete each sentence about the podcast to which you listened.

1. The thing I liked best about your podcast was . . .

_____

_____

2. Something you could do to improve your podcast is . . .

_____

_____

3. What I learned from your podcast was . . .

_____

_____

4. Answers to your five questions:

_____

_____

_____

Step by Step

In this multi-day activity, students practice developing sentences literally one step at a time. Using cutout footprints, students practice elaborating their thoughts and varying sentence structure by adding nouns, verbs, adjectives, adverbs, conjunctions, prepositional phrases, and introductory elements step by step.

This activity is not easy to do, yet, surprisingly enough, students do get the hang of this. Once they do, this activity can be used to describe anything from fictional characters to content-area concepts. Of course, you will use only the footprints and the sentence-structure skills that are appropriate for your grade level.

MATERIALS:
Paper
Pens/pencils
Eight (or fewer) footprints
Reading material, if needed

This activity builds new sentence concepts throughout several days. Because it takes only a few minutes, it fits well at the beginning or end of class.

Depending upon the readiness of the students, you might only choose to teach several days' lessons with students only completing several footprints.

At the beginning of the school year, most fourth-grade students can complete this activity through day 5. Days 6 through 8 can be added later in the school year when students are comfortable writing compound sentences and are ready to become more mature writers.

One suggested procedure for middle-school students:
- day 1 nouns and verbs
- day 2 adjectives and adverbs
- day 3 prepositional phrases
- day 4 the comma/conjunction rule
- day 5 reviews what was previously taught
- day 6 subordinate clauses
- day 7 participle phrases
- day 8 one introductory element added to the sentence to the right of the conjunction

Model each concept as you teach or review it. Then ask each student to provide his own example that illustrates the skill being taught. Included below are several excellent books by Brian P. Cleary about the parts of speech that can be used to introduce the grammatical concept for that day.

DIRECTIONS:
Students will need eight template copies of a footprint, numbered 1–8. You can supply these, or students can trace their own footprints and cut them out. They will complete one footprint each day.

Step by Step (continued)

Below is a day-by-day explanation of the eight concepts suitable for middle school.

Day 1: Define what a sentence is by explaining to students that a complete sentence must have a noun and a verb and express a complete thought. Excellent resources to review nouns and verbs are Brian P. Cleary's books *A Mink, a Fink, a Skating Rink: What Is a Noun?* and *To Root, to Toot, to Parachute: What Is a Verb?* After this, instruct each student to write a two-word sentence with a noun and a verb on footprint #1. Students are allowed to use the word *the* to begin the sentence. (Jane travels.)

Day 2: Provide a brief mini-lesson on adjectives and adverbs. Brian P. Cleary's books *Hairy, Scary, Ordinary: What Is an Adjective?* and *Dearly, Nearly, Insincerely: What Is an Adverb?* are excellent resources to review these concepts. Students are then instructed to add an adjective and an adverb to their noun/verb sentences on footprint #2. Students can change tenses as needed. (Curious Jane traveled slowly.)

Day 3: Provide a brief mini-lesson about prepositional phrases. You can begin this lesson by asking a student volunteer to stand **by** a desk, go **under** the desk, walk **around** the desk, get **near** the desk, etc., to illustrate that prepositions usually indicate space or time. Brian P. Cleary's book *Under, Over, By the Clover: What Is a Preposition?* is also an excellent resource to teach this concept. You will also need to provide examples of prepositional phrases. Then instruct students to add a prepositional phrase to the noun and a prepositional phrase to the verb in sentence #2 on footprint #3. (In the summer, curious Jane traveled slowly across the country.)

Day 4: Provide a brief mini-lesson about the comma/conjunction rule, which states that two independent clauses joined by a coordinating conjunction (*and, or, but, for, yet*) are joined by a comma placed before the conjunction. Provide several examples and non-examples of this rule.

Example: The girls went to the party, and they had fun.
Out in the forest, a tree fell, and it crashed to Earth.

Non-example: The girls went to a party and had fun.
Out in the forest a tree fell and crashed to Earth.

On footprint #4, students create two independent clauses joined by a conjunction. The second sentence should contain a noun and a verb. Students can use the word *the*. (In the summer, curious Jane traveled slowly across the country, and the car broke.)

Days 5 and 6: Students have just learned how to develop a sentence by adding an adjective to describe the noun, an adverb to describe the verb, and to add prepositional phrases. On footprint #4 students created a compound sentence by adding the comma/conjunction and another two- or three-word sentence. For footprints #5 and #6, students repeat the steps completed in footprints #2 and #3, adding an adjective and adverb to this new sentence after the comma/conjunction on footprint #5 and adding two prepositional phrases on footprint #6. Students can use their previous footprints as a model to follow.

Step by Step (continued)

(#5: In the summer, curious Jane traveled slowly across the country, and the old car broke down.)

(#6: In the summer, curious Jane traveled slowly across the country, and in the mountains the old car broke down near a cliff.)

Days 7 and 8: Students will now learn to develop sentences by adding introductory elements. Two mini-lessons will need to be taught: one explaining subordinate clauses and one explaining participle phrases. You can do an online search for subordinate clauses and participle phrases to find many good examples.

Examples of subordinate clauses: Because I'm hungry,
Although I stayed up late,

Examples of participle phrases: Running out onto the field,
Cheering for their team,

Once students can write these introductory elements, footprint #7 will add one introductory element to the sentence to the left of the conjunction, and footprint #8 will add one introductory element to the sentence to the right of the conjunction.

(#7: Going on a vacation in the summer, curious Jane traveled slowly across the country, and in the mountains, the old car broke down near a cliff.)

(#8: Going on a vacation in the summer, curious Jane traveled slowly across the country, and riding along in the mountains, the old car broke down near a cliff.)

Footprints Developed from a Science Unit about Volcanoes: Volcanoes erupt.

- Shield volcanoes erupt slowly.
- Shield volcanoes in Hawaii erupt slowly down the mountain.
- Shield volcanoes in Hawaii erupt slowly down the mountain, and the land changes.
- Shield volcanoes in Hawaii erupt slowly down the mountain, and the scenic land slowly changes.
- Shield volcanoes in Hawaii erupt slowly down the mountain, and the scenic land around the volcano slowly changes over time.
- When the enormous pressure of the hot magma increases, shield volcanoes in Hawaii erupt slowly down the mountain, and the scenic land around the volcano slowly changes over time.
- When the enormous pressure of the hot magma inside the Earth increases to a certain level, shield volcanoes in Hawaii erupt slowly down the mountain, and the scenic land around the volcano slowly changes over time.

Think-Pair-Share with a Movie

Think-pair-share is typically considered a strategy used for print. But why not apply it when viewing a movie, too? This engaging activity provides a springboard for discussion about short movies and helps students learn to "read" them.

MATERIALS:
Movie (DVD)
Paper
Pencils

DIRECTIONS:
Select a movie that would interest your students. The movie might tie in with a literature unit or a unit of study.

Stop the movie at various points and allow students to discuss what they viewed with partners. Encourage them to ask questions of their partner to clear up questions about what they viewed.

Once the movie ends, students discuss information about the movie with their partners, focusing on questions like these:

FICTION

- What did you think of the characters?
- Who was the protagonist? Can you make any personal connections to this character?
- Who was the antagonist? Can you make any personal connections to this character?
- How did the setting affect the story? Have you ever been to a place like this?
- If you could change the setting of the selection, where might it take place?
- What was the major problem in the selection? Have you ever encountered such a problem?
- What events led up to the climax?
- What was the resolution? Could the problem have been solved in another way?
- What might have been a better ending to the selection?

NON-FICTION

- What were the major concepts discussed?
- How does the material in the video relate to what we have been studying in class?
- What did you learn about the topic that you didn't already know?

Some Good Short Movies:

- *Scorpions* by Walter Dean Myers
- *The Veldt* by Ray Bradbury
- *The Ransom of Red Chief* by O. Henry
- *The Adventure of the Speckled Band* adapted from the story by Arthur Conan Doyle
- *The Tell-Tale Heart* by Edgar Allan Poe
- *The Monkey's Paw* by W.W. Jacobs
- *The Necklace* by Guy de Maupassant
- *The Celebrated Jumping Frog of Calaveras County* by Mark Twain
- All science videos by Bill Nye the Science Guy
- National Geographic videos

⊙ *Teacher Tip*

Many video clips on YouTube are produced by students. After they see a few of them, your students might want to produce their own video based on a selection they have read.

Tic-Tac-Toe Facts

Tic-Tac-Toe Facts makes concept review fun. Create the boards yourself, or allow students to make them.

MATERIALS:
Tic-tac-toe board
Answer key
Pens/pencils

DIRECTIONS:
Prepare a nine-sectioned tic-tac-toe board. Each square should hold one question or statement to which students should respond by applying the missing punctuation.. See completed example on the following page.

Prepare an answer key for the game, and make it available to students to use to check their answers after they complete a game. If you prefer, you can check answers.

This game is played just like the traditional tic-tac-toe: the objective is to get three answers correct horizontally or vertically. The first student to do this with all correct answers is the winner.

Put the students into pairs. The first student to go responds to one section on the game board. He also places his initials on his completed section. Student two goes next.

When one student thinks he has tic-tac-toe, the student pair then checks the answers on the answer key. If correct, the game ends. If the declaring student's answers were not all correct, the game continues until one student has tic-tac-toe. Most often the games go by quickly, taking no more than five minutes.

Variations:

Students can create the tic-tac-toe boards along with the answer keys, and students can play each other's games.

A student can also play alone, selecting one row or column to complete. The game can be turned into a contest to see which student gets tic-tac-toe first. After one student gets tic-tac-toe and the teacher checks his game board, students can continue to play to see who can get all four corners. After a winner is announced for this game, students can play to see who can complete the entire game board correctly.

Punctuation Tic-Tac-Toe

DIRECTIONS:

One student responds to one section on the game board and places his initials on the corresponding section. The other student repeats this process. When one of you thinks you have tic-tac-toe, you can check your answers on the answer key or see the teacher.

In the middle of the road I saw a raccoon	Don't run too fast you might hurt yourself	I went to visit the Grand Canyon in Arizona
My favorite foods are spaghetti tacos and pizza	At the beginning of the school year students have many concepts to learn	The childrens toys were scattered all about
Do you think asked Loni that we can go to the movies	The train leaves the station at 900 am	There arent many students who like to do homework

To Tell the Truth

When you engage students in learning facts about a unit of study in a game format, everyone wins! In this activity, students prepare true and false statements about a topic of study. Working with a partner or in a small group, students read a statement and determine whether it is true or false. Students respond to this competitive game by creating challenging questions to stymie their classmates.

MATERIALS:

Paper

Pens/pencils

Literary or content-area material

DIRECTIONS:

Ask each student to write five statements about a reading selection or a topic of study. Tell them that some statements should be true and some should be false.

Once their questions are written, pair students. The first partner reads a statement, and her partner must guess whether it is true or false. If the answer is right, the partner then asks his question.

If an answer is not correct, the partners discuss the question with the questioner showing where the answer appears in the text. The game then continues until all five questions have been answered.

If time permits, students can switch partners.

Collect all questions and select those you deem appropriate to use when it's time to assess the material taught.

◉ *Teacher Tip*

To vary the activity, select four or five students to sit in front of the room as a panel. Students in the audience who have written their questions quiz panel members. When a student misses a question, he returns to his seat and the person asking the question joins the panel. Before the questions continue, the new panel member must answer the question that was missed.

Two-Column Notes

This graphic organizer allows students to share their interpretations of text and to make personal connections. Reading becomes personal when connections are made to text. And, when students have an opportunity to share their connections, those responses trigger even more connections.

MATERIALS:

Two-column notes graphic organizer for students
to copy onto their own papers
Paper
Pencils
Text chunks from study selection

DIRECTIONS:

This activity can be used during or after reading a selection or content-area material.

Review the **Two-Column Notes Example** on p. 64. Divide students into small groups of three or four students. Each group creates a simple two-columned chart on a piece of paper, labeled as follows:

<u>**What the Text Says**</u>	<u>**What the Text Means to Me**</u>

Students place a copy of the text to be discussed on the top of their charts. Each group can be given the same or a different chunk of text to which they should make connections. Students can copy this from their books, or it can be placed on the document camera, whiteboard, or overhead.

Students in each group discuss their chunks of text and make personal connections to the text. Each student places his initials on the chart following his personal response.

Provide time for each group to respond and discuss the rationale for group members' responses.

Once students have completed making the connections in their small groups, allow the groups to share their sentences or chunks of text and the connections made with the whole class.

Two-Column Notes

EXAMPLE

FROM "A BACKWOODS BOY" BY RUSSELL FREEDMAN

What the Text Says	*What the Text Means to Me*
Abraham passed his eighth birthday in the lean-to. He was big for his age, a "tall spider of a boy," and old enough to handle an ax. He helped his father clear the land. They planted corn and pumpkin seeds between the tree stumps. And they built a new log cabin, the biggest one yet, where Abraham climbed a ladder and slept in a loft beneath the roof.	I'm big for my age and skinny. (JT)
	My dad won't let me hold an ax or any power tools. He said I'm not old enough. (KW)
	I help my dad mow the yard. (LR)
	My mom and I plant a garden. (KT)
	My parents had a new house built. (DP)
	I wish I were tall for my age! (HC)
	My dad and I put up a shed. (SR)
	My bedroom is upstairs. I'm glad I don't have to climb a ladder to get up there. (MB)

Vocabulary Connections

Students acquire new vocabulary when they can make personal connections to the new words. This two-day activity allows students to play with new words so that the words become their own.

MATERIALS:

Paper
Pencils
A list of vocabulary words

DIRECTIONS:

Using a list of vocabulary words from a unit of study, each student writes one question or statement for every word (see the examples below). These will be written on a sheet of paper with statements or questions on separate lines to allow room for responses.

Collect the completed statements or questions. On the following day, distribute the papers so that each student completes someone else's paper.

Discuss responses.

Variation:

Select several of the students' statements or questions, and write each individual question or statement on a sheet of chart paper. Post the chart paper in various locations around the room, and allow students to walk quietly around the room and respond to the statements on the chart paper. Instruct students to place their initials beside their responses.

Sample Questions/Statements:

- Missions that have gone awry
- Places that are ubiquitous
- People who might be jaunty
- People who are haggard
- People who may need a proxy
- People who are aloof
- When might a person be unflagging?
- When might a person be stoic?
- When might you need to have tenacity?

⊙ *Teacher Tip*

- *When students make*
- *personal connections to*
- *vocabulary words, the words*
- *become more meaningful.*
- *Being able to make*
- *connections to new words*
- *allows students to think at*
- *higher cognitive levels.*

Vocabulary Poetry

In this two-day activity, students make connections to vocabulary words by developing several descriptive definitions of each word as poems. Students retain more words when they work with them over and over.

MATERIALS:

Paper
Pens/pencils
A list of vocabulary words

DIRECTIONS:

Show students a model of a vocabulary poem (see next page).

Ask students to select a vocabulary word from the list you are working with for that week and write a poem describing the word. The poem's first word will be the vocabulary word; the following five or six lines should provide examples that describe the word.

When students finish, collect all poems.

For the next day's activity, select at least one poem that defines each vocabulary word. Selecting more than one poem for each word makes the activity more difficult.

Cut and past the poems on a sheet of copy paper. Number each poem.

Make one copy of the collection of poems. This will be your answer key.

On the original copy of the poems, white out the vocabulary word in each poem. This should be the first word of each poem.

To do this activity, you can provide each student with a copy of the poems, or you can display them on the whiteboard. If students have a copy of the poems, they read each poem and write the vocabulary word in the blanked out space. If they are reading the poems from the whiteboard, they will write the number of each poem on a sheet of paper with the corresponding vocabulary word.

While doing this activity, students may look at their vocabulary lists.

Discuss answers.

Teacher Tip

"A robust approach to vocabulary involves directly explaining the meanings of words along with thought-provoking, playful, and interactive follow-up."

Isabel Beck, 2002

Vocabulary Poetry
EXAMPLE

_____ is unmoving and cold

He's the image of self control

The guards that don't speak

Statues in the square

Impassive and stony

He watches the people on the street

He has no friends, no companions

You might even say he doesn't feel a thing.

(answer: *stoic*)

_____ is tacky, showy, and tasteless

Like a tourist in a Hawaiian print shirt

Like a pop star showing too much skin

Like glitter and rainbows

And print on print

Like socks with sandals

Don't fit.

(answer: *tawdry*)

Web Quest Challenge
AN ONLINE SCAVENGER HUNT

Build background knowledge and strengthen connections to a topic of study with this online scavenger hunt. Students use online sources to locate information about a topic of study—with a fun twist: each student must locate a *different* fact about the topic. No two students can write the same fact. If online resources are not available, students can find research facts in the media center.

MATERIALS:

Internet access
Reference/research sources
Paper
Pens/pencils
Sentence strips
Tape

DIRECTIONS:

Students find one fact about a specified topic of study using online sources.

The first student who completes the Web Quest Challenge writes his fact on a sentence strip that is posted, initialing his find on the strip.

As each student finds his fact, he must first check to see whether his fact has already been found. If it has, he must go back to the Internet or another source and find a different fact. If his fact is not posted, he writes the fact on a sentence strip and posts it under the others.

Provide time for all students to find a fact.

⊙ *Teacher Tip*

- *Web Quest Challenge*
- *really works to motivate*
- *struggling students. After*
- *the first game, you might*
- *notice that the students who*
- *normally hang back until an*
- *assignment is almost over*
- *will be the first to find and*
- *post a fact.*

EXAMPLE: HOLOCAUST WEB QUEST

- Six million Jews were killed. (JT)

- 1933: Hitler became chancellor of Germany. (AS)

- Final Solution: Hitler's systematic plan to attempt to annihilate the entire Jewish population of Europe (IF)

- Nuremberg Laws, Sept. 15, 1935: The legal basis for the Jews' exclusion from German society; a policy that restricted Jewish people (WD)

- Jews were forced into crowded ghettos isolated from the rest of society. (EG)

- Kristallnacht, Nov. 9–10, 1935: The night of broken glass; Nazis looted and destroyed Jews' homes and businesses and burned their synagogues. (NS)

- Warsaw ghetto uprising: The largest ghetto revolt; the Jews withstood the Germans for 27 days.

- Three million Jews were murdered in Poland. (AF)

- Jews were forced to wear badges marking them as Jews. (NW)

- Three and a half million Jews were murdered in death camps. (FM)

- Dachau, near Munich, was the first concentration camp built in 1933. (GW)

- Gas chambers were built in six concentration camps in Poland to systematically murder the Jews. (AP)

- A wide range of victim groups suffered under the Nazis including Communists, Jehovah's Witnesses, Romani, and homosexuals. (BW)

Writing on the Wall

This activity allows students to respond to fiction or non-fiction by writing on each other's "wall" just as they do on Facebook. (Just mentioning Facebook is a motivator!) Students are able to share their interpretations of a reading selection by "talking" on paper. According to researcher Edgar Dale (1956), students remember 70 percent of what they talk about with others.

MATERIALS:

Paper
Pens/pencils
Reading material

DIRECTIONS:

After reading a fiction or non-fiction text selection, each student writes a statement or question about what they read on the top of a piece of notebook paper. This becomes the student's wall.

Each student then responds to his statement or question and passes his paper to the next student who responds to the previous student's answer. Each new response should include a detail from the selection or unit of study. A response that includes an unsupported statement or opinion is not permitted.

Students continue passing the papers around the room together to gather as many responses as time permits.

Collect all papers.

Place students in groups of about five or six, and provide each group with one paper. Allow students to read and discuss responses. Do they agree with the conversation on paper? Is there anything with which they do not agree? Can they provide other details from the selection to support what was stated?

After students complete discussions on one paper, give them another. When at least one group has discussed everyone's papers, work with the class to create a chart of common points students raised.

Example from "The Story of an Hour" by Kate Chopin:

Student 1:   This story is about a girl who is told her husband is dead. She believes she is now free. Then her husband comes home, and she dies of shock.

Student 2:   Well, the theme of the story is to expect the unexpected.

Student 3:   It was ironic how she was happy when she found out about his death instead of mourning his death.

Student 4:   So, do you guys think he really loved her?

Student 5:   Yes, because it said he was smothering her.

Student 6:   I think they loved each other but weren't in love with each other. Kind of sad that she died having never really felt freedom.

Student 7:   Yes, I agree. She felt that his love was more smothering than caring. It's ironic how everything turned out. Don't you think?

Student 8:   Indeed. When he died, she felt relieved in a way because she gained freedom.

Student 9:   I mean she was all happy, and then she goes "Aww, man!" when she sees her husband.

Student 10: I think she just died of a heart attack. It was the transfer from joy to disappointment that initiated it.

Example from *Freak the Mighty* by Rodman Philbrick:

Student 1:   Max and Kevin are lucky they found each other.

Student 2:   Yeah, with both of them being weird, they're lucky to each have a good friend.

Student 3:   I don't know why a smart kid like Freak wants to hang with a doofus like Max.

Student 4:   Max might be a doofus, but he's cool.

Student 5:   Why do you think Max is cool?

Student 6:   He lives in the Down Under and that's cool. He is also willing to go on all of Freak's adventures.

Student 7:   Yeah, Max first appears to be a scaredy cat, but he's really a good friend.

Student 8:   My friend, Shawn, is like Max. He's afraid to do some stuff 'cause he thinks he'll get in trouble, but he's always there for me, and we have fun together.

Student 9:   Max is always there for Kevin.

Student 10: And Kevin's always there for Max.

Who Said It?

In this activity, students practice determining a character's tone, voice, and mood using quotes from a reading selection and share their interpretations with others. They support their opinions from examples in the text. Who Said It? can be used as a whole-class activity, with everyone responding to the same quote, or with partners or in small groups by assigning different quotes.

DIRECTIONS:

Select quotes from a reading selection. Type the quotes and cite the page number where the quote is found.

If all students will be responding to the same quote, you will need a copy of the quote for each student. This quote can be written on the board or placed on the document camera for students to copy.

If students will be working with partners or in small groups, each person in the group or each partner will need a copy of the same quote. To do this, print one quote for each person or group member. Each individual quote will be printed on a different colored sheet of copy paper.

Randomly distribute the quotes. The activity begins with each student working independently to respond to the quote he received.

Each student reads the quote and responds on a sheet of paper using details from the selection to support the response. Student should tell who is speaking and describe the character's tone of voice and mood. The cited page number will help the students read what happens before and after the quote to determine the answers.

Once students have finished their responses, it's time to get together with another person or a small group of students who responded to the same quote. Students get together with others who have quotes printed on the same colored paper. The students then exchange papers, read that response, and react to it, providing a rationale for their opinions based on the text. Whether they agree or disagree with what the other person wrote, they must provide details from the text supporting their opinions.

Color-coding Suggestions:

- Print quotes on different colored paper
- Print quotes and place a colored dot on similar quotes
- Print quotes and place the quote in a plastic snack bag that is color coded
- Print quotes and place similar stickers on similar quotes

After about twenty minutes of sharing, display all the quotes on a document camera, whiteboard, or overhead, and provide time for more discussion, if desired.

Variation:

Allow students to partner with someone who has a different quote and respond to this person's response.

Example from "The Drummer Boy of Shiloh" by Ray Bradbury

Quote: "Well," said the voice quietly, "here's a soldier crying *before* the fight. Good. Get it over. Won't be time once it all starts."

Student's Response to the Quote:

Joby is a drummer boy in the Civil War. Drummer boys carry no weapons, only their drums. Joby is scared. The general speaking to him lets him know how important he is to the battle. He will set the pace of the battle. If the drum beats slowly, then the men's hearts would beat slowly, and the enemy would stop them. He tells Joby that he is the heart of the army. You can tell that Joby respects this man and looks up to him as a father figure. He mentions that the man smells as all fathers should smell. He helps to calm Joby.

Another Student's Response to This Response:

I, too, would be scared if I knew I was going into a war with just a drum in my hand. With so many men nervous and unable to sleep, it was really kind of the general to stop to spend time and comfort Joby. Joby looked upon the general as a father figure. He must have respected his father as he respects this general. He tells Joby that one day he will look back at this experience and be proud that he was a part of the battle of Owl Creek.

More Active Vocabulary Activities

TV/Book/Product
Use vocabulary words to make a TV/book/product advertisement.

Crossword Puzzle
Have students create a crossword puzzle/answer key using vocabulary words. Trade and complete.

Words in Print Display
Encourage students to find vocabulary words in print. Cut or copy one sentence or more using the vocabulary word to create a Words in Print display. This is an excellent way to display word wall words as they are used in context.

Improv Theatre
Use vocabulary words for an improv theater. One or two students select a word from a bucket or bag. Give the student(s) one minute to decide how to act out the word. The audience must guess the word being acted out. Students can also be placed in small groups with each group preparing a skit using as many vocabulary words as they can from their lists. Students can place word cards on their backs with the words they are acting out.

Cartoons/Storyboard
Have students create cartoons or storyboards using vocabulary words.

About Me
Students describe themselves, a peer, a character in a story, a person from history, a scientist, or a parent using designated vocabulary words.

Words in Writing
Encourage students to use their vocabulary words when writing. Instruct them to highlight or underline each vocabulary word used in the writing piece. You can also require students to use a set number of words and include this as part of the grading rubric.

Labeling Images
Instruct students to cut pictures out of magazines that describe vocabulary words. They can write the word directly on the picture.

Place art exemplars or prints around the room, and ask students to write and place descriptive vocabulary words on sticky notes on the art.

More Active Reading Strategies

Personally Speaking

Students create a Venn diagram to help them make personal connections to the text they are reading. Some examples: Compare an animal in a selection to the student's pet. Compare/contrast a character to a family member or friend.

Sticky Questions

As students read a text selection, encourage them to use sticky notes to ask questions when they are not sure of the meaning. As students find the answers to their questions, they move the sticky note to the section of the text where they find the answer. Unanswered questions are discussed with the class or with partners.

Chunk to Conquer

To help visualize and master difficult text, use chunking. Chunk a fiction or non-fiction selection into eight smaller sections, and provide each student with a sheet of 12" x 18" construction paper. Students fold the paper in half, then in half again, and in half once more to create eight sections. Students illustrate each chunk of text on one of the eight sections. Provide time for students to share their illustrations with a partner. Display.

Questions, Questions

Lessons become games when each student writes five questions about a text selection. Divide the class into teams and display the questions on a document camera or whiteboard, if available. Teams take turns trying to answer questions correctly. To make this more challenging, require students to develop one question from each level of Bloom's Taxonomy or Webb's Depth of Knowledge.

React!

Reaction journals provide a good way for students to record their emotions after they read a text selection. A simple mini-book (see directions on p. 78) created from a 12" x 18" piece of paper makes an excellent journal.

Take a Picture

Photo journals allow students to write a summary of a chunked piece of text and illustrate it. Text can be chunked by paragraph, page, or chapter. Students illustrate the main idea and provide a summary sentence. This is another good use for the mini-book.

Chunk a Lesson

After ten to fifteen minutes of instruction, place students in small groups of four or five students and give each group a piece of chart paper. Each group writes down facts they learned during the lesson. Before you resume the lesson, allow students to share their responses.

PART THREE

Mini-book and Fortune Teller Templates

"Good teaching is more of giving the right questions than a giving of right answers."

– JOSEF ALBERS, EDUCATOR

Mini-book Templates

The mini-book concept is extremely versatile and easy to create. The engaging mini-books can be used to respond to fiction or non-fiction, to practice reading and writing strategies, or to learn vocabulary, figurative language, and conventions. After you create a few from the following templates, you will think of many more ways to incorporate them into your teaching day. Mini-books are a naturally differentiated teaching tool.

CREATING THE MINI-BOOK FROM THE TEMPLATES:

Copy the templates.

1. Students fold the selected mini-book in half, in half again, and once more to create eight sections.

2. Unfold the paper, and fold it in half so that one 8 ½" side meets the other 8 ½" side (hamburger fold). Cut on the fold from the center to the middle of the paper. Open the paper.

3. Now fold the paper so that one 11" side meets the other 11" side (hotdog fold).

4. Hold the paper with one hand on each 8 ½" side and push in and fold around into a mini-book. The text will be facing you.

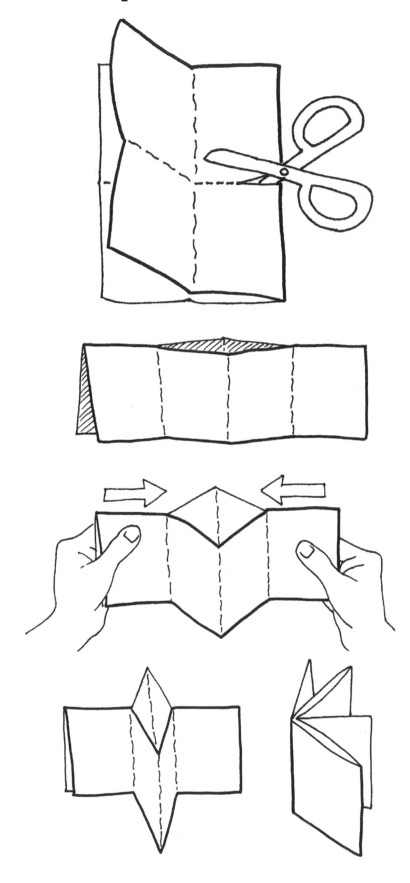

MINI-BOOK TEMPLATE

A Novel: Chapter by Chapter

Students respond to literary elements as they read a novel.

During Reading

What confuses you?
What questions do you have?

During Reading

What problems (conflicts) arise?

During Reading

Visualize what this chapter is about by drawing a picture.

During Reading

Is the problem solved?
If so, tell how.

Book Title

Chapter #: _____

Title: _____

Predict what this chapter is going to be about.

After Reading

What is the main idea of this chapter?

BACK PAGE

After Reading

What do you think will happen in the next story?

Make a prediction.

MINI-BOOK TEMPLATE

Applying Reading Strategies

Students apply reading strategies as they read a fiction or non-fiction selection. The focus is on visualizing, making connections, making predictions, and questioning the text.

Make Connections:

Make a personal connection to something you read in the text.

Predictions:

Stop at one point in the text and predict what will happen.

Visualize:

Create an illustration for something you read in the reading selection.

Predictions:

How accurate was your prediction? If not the same as yours, explain what did happen.

Applying Reading Strategies

Selection read:

Questioning the Text:

Write down questions you have as you read.

Questioning the Text:

If your questions were answered, write the answers. If not, discuss your questions with a friend.

BACK PAGE

MINI-BOOK TEMPLATE

Before/During/After Reading Strategies

Differentiate instruction by allowing students to choose activities to complete before, during, and after reading.

During Reading

- Learning log
- Make predictions
- Questions I have
- Vocabulary I don't know
- Illustrations
- Notes to the characters (dialogue journal)
- Sticky notes
- Interesting facts
- What's not clear
- Create a story board of important ideas
- Double entry journal: Place a phrase or sentence in the left column; in the right column tell what this phrase or sentence means to you
- Reciprical teaching
  - Predicting
  - Clarifying
  - Questioning
  - Summarizing
  - Think-pair-share

- What is the purpose for reading?
- What do the illustrations tell you about the story?
- What does the title tell you about the selection?
- If there are bold print headings, what do these tell you about the selection?

Before Reading

- Concept maps
- Activating prior knowledge
- K-D-L (what I know, what I don't know, what I learned)
- Anticipation guides
- A hook: movie clip, YouTube video, related children's book
- A to Z with words related to the topic of study
- Anticipation box: Place artifacts in a box; pull out one at a time while students predict what will happen in the story

After Reading

- QAR's (Question-Answer-Relationships)
- Herringbone graphic organizer
- Add to the A to Z chart
- Retelling to a partner
- One sentence summary
- Letter to the author telling what you liked or did not like about the selection/story
- Plot poems
- Nonfiction: Create a commemorative stamp for each person in the selection
- Create a milk carton showing one literary element on each side with an illustration
- Questions for each category of Bloom's taxonomy in the form of a flip book. Students write and answer their questions or trade questions with another student
  - Remembering
  - Understanding
  - Applying
  - Analyzing
  - Evaluating
  - Creating
- Assign sections of the story to small groups and have students act out scenes
- Create a business card for any character

Before During After Reading Strategies

BACK PAGE

MINI-BOOK TEMPLATE

One Word, Many Cognitive Levels

Activities at each level of Bloom's Taxonomy challenge students to think more deeply as they make connections to their vocabulary words. You can assign just one word for students to focus on, with students sharing mini-books with others. Or, each student can create one mini-book for all the assigned vocabulary words.

Comprehension/Understand:
Write a definition in your own words

Applications/Apply:
Use the word in a complete sentence

Knowledge/remember:
Define the word

Analysis/Analyze:
Provide an example and a non-example

One Word, Many Cognitive Levels

My Word:

My Name:

Evaluation/Evaluate:
Provide a linear array using your word

(i.e.: big, huge, gigantic, everywhere, omnipresent, ubiquitous)

Synthesis/Create:
Create a song, rap, or cartoon using this word

BACK PAGE

MINI-BOOK TEMPLATE

Extended Thinking 1: Making Connections

Students are encouraged to respond to fiction selections at higher cognitive levels and make connections as they compare and contrast and analyze characters.

How would you have dealt with the antagonist if you were the protagonist?

Compare and contrast yourself to someone you know or to a character in the selection you are reading.

How is the main conflict in this selection similar to another conflict in history?

Extended Thinking I

Analyzing Characters

BACK PAGE

MINI-BOOK TEMPLATE

Extended Thinking 2: Characterization, Point of View, and Setting

Students analyze literary elements to extend their thinking beyond the text for characterization, point of view, and setting.

From whose point of view is this selection told? How would the story be different if it was told from another point of view?

Create a metaphor, a similie, and an analogy to describe a character you are reading about.

What are the advantages and disadvantages of the setting of this selection?

Extended Thinking II

Characterization

Point of view

Setting

BACK PAGE

MINI-BOOK TEMPLATE

Extended Thinking 3: Conflict, Characterization, and Theme

Students analyze literary elements to extend their thinking beyond the text for conflict, characterization, and theme.

What might have gone wrong if the protagonist had made a different choice when solving the conflict?

Which fact from your reading provides the best evidence that a conflict was about to begin?

What details led to this story's theme?

Extended Thinking III

Conflict

Characterization

Theme

BACK PAGE

MINI-BOOK TEMPLATE

Figurative Language Scavenger Hunt

Students gain valuable practice with finding similes, metaphors, and personification in their texts. If the scavenger hunt doesn't yield all the examples you have assigned, students can write their own examples.

Metaphor

Locate a metaphor, write the metaphor, and tell what is being compared.

Write your own simile and tell what is being compared.

Simile

Locate a simile, write the simile and tell what is being compared.

Write your own metaphor and tell what is being compared.

Personification

Locate an example of personification, write the example and explain.

Figurative Language Scavenger Hunt

Directions

1. Find the example of the figurative language requested.
2. Tell the book and page number where you found your example.
3. Follow the directions on each page.

Write your own example of personification and explain.

MINI-BOOK TEMPLATE

Introductory Elements

Students practice sentence variation with subordinate clauses, prepositional phrases, and participle phrases. Ask students to first define the introductory element if they can. Once you provide examples, they can either revise their own answers or write in the correct definition along with an example. Space is provided to add examples, a main clause, and an introductory element.

Two Prepositional Phrases

a. Define prepositional phrase

b. Redefine prepositional phrase

c. Examples of prepositional phrases

d. Add a main clause to two prepositional phrases to make a sentence

Subordinating Conjunctions

Prepositions

Subordinate Clause

a. Define

b. Refine definition

c. Examples of subordinate clauses (underline subordinating conjunction)

d. Add a main clause to a subordinate clause to make a sentence

Participle Phrases

a. Define

b. Redefine

c. Examples of participle phrases

d. Add a main clause to one participle phrase to make a sentence

Introductory Elements

Participles

BACK PAGE

MINI-BOOK TEMPLATE

Literary Analysis

Students respond to literary elements from any fiction selection. The focus is on character development, setting, point of view, plot development, and conflict/resolution.

Point of View

Tell how one character feels about another character. Provide details from the selection to support your answer.

Setting

Explain why the setting is important to this selection.

Character Development

Select one character in the selection and tell how this character changes from the beginning to the end of the selection.

Plot Development

List three important events in the plot development. Tell why each is significant.

Literary Analysis

Problem

What is the main problem in this selection?

Resolution

Tell how the main problem is solved.

Book Title

Your Name

MINI-BOOK TEMPLATE

Reading Comprehension

Author's purpose, main idea and details, cause/effect, text structure, and compare/contrast are covered in this mini-book, which can be used with both fiction and non-fiction selections.

Main Idea

What is the main idea of this selection?

Main Idea/Details

List three details from the selection to support the main idea.

Author's Purpose

Why do you think the author wrote this selection?

Cause/Effect

Provide one cause and its effect based on one character's actions.

Reading Comprehension

Text Structure

How is the information in this selection organized? Check one.

- ☐ Sequence of events
- ☐ Listing / descriptions
- ☐ Spatial order
- ☐ Compare / contrast
- ☐ Cause / effect
- ☐ Question / answer
- ☐ Definition / explanation
- ☐ To provide evidence

Compare/Contrast

Tell how two characters in the selection are alike and how they are different.

BACK PAGE

Fortune Teller Templates

Fortune tellers allow you an engaging way to review any academic subject while the students are having fun! Begin by using the completed templates in this book, then let the students create their own. (A blank template that notes placement of the questions and answers is included.) Students like to take the fortune tellers home, too, to play with friends and family members.

DIRECTIONS: HOW TO ASSEMBLE THE FORTUNE TELLER TEMPLATE

1. Cut one template from the book around the dark edges. You will have a square.

2. Fold the paper from one corner and crease.

3. Fold the paper again so that the opposite corners meet. Crease. You now have a crease in the shape of an X running through the center.

4. Laying the square of paper flat on a table, fold each corner into the center.

5. Turn the paper over, and fold each corner into the center.

6. Fold the paper in half with the flaps that are sticking up folded into the center. To make the fortune teller more pliable, fold it in half in the opposite direction.

7. Place your fingers into the openings, and move your fingers to open and close the fortune teller.

If students create their own fortune tellers, begin with a sheet of 8 ½" by 11" paper. Students first fold the paper from corner to corner. They then cut off the excess paper so they are left with a square. Follow directions above, beginning with #2.

How to Use the Fortune Teller for Practicing Word Parts with a Partner:

- To use the fortune teller, students spell out any word, prefix, or suffix on the top of the fortune teller, moving the fortune teller one time by opening and closing it for each letter in the word, prefix, or suffix.

- To play, place students into pairs. One student selects one word written on the exterior flap of his partner's fortune teller. The partner then opens and closes his fortune teller as many times as there are letters in the chosen word or word part.

- The first student selects and answers one of the four questions visible on the interior segments of the fortune teller.

- The student must respond to the question or statement and check his answer under the question or statement flap.

- Now it's the other student's turn.

- If students want to play for points, students give each other one point for each question or statement answered correctly.

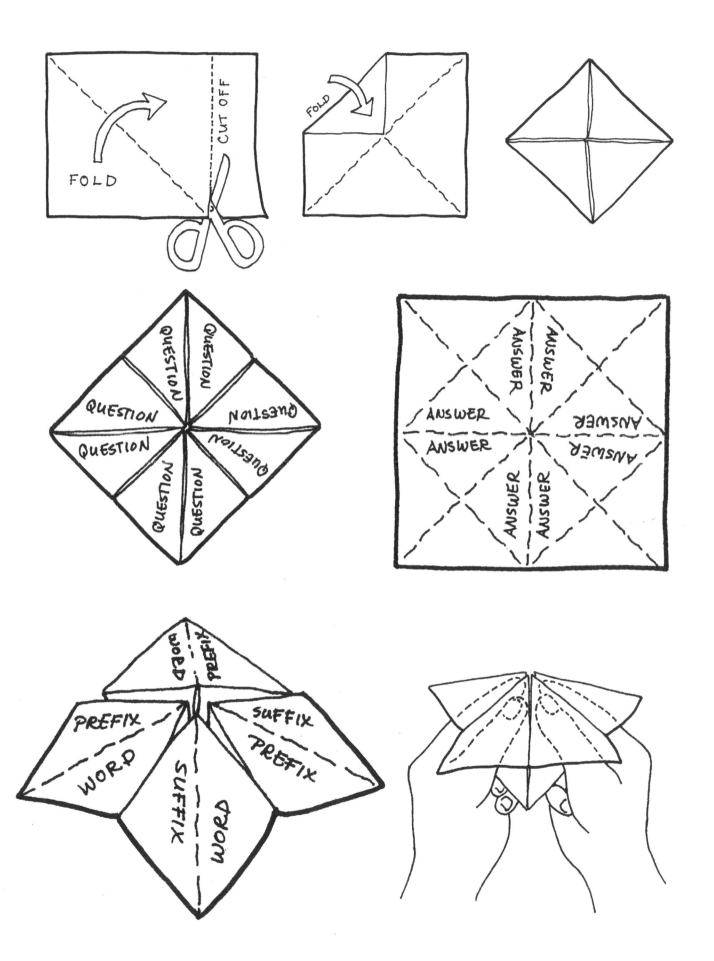

FORTUNE TELLER TEMPLATE

Blank Fortune Teller Template

Students can have fun creating their own fortune tellers using academic content from any unit of study. The template notes where to place questions and answers.

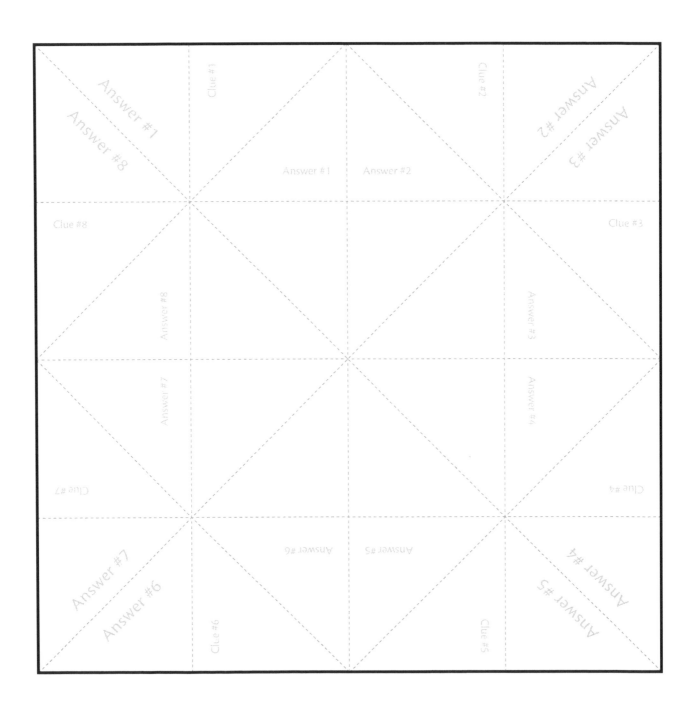

FORTUNE TELLER TEMPLATE

Fiction Frenzy

This fortune teller can be used with any book or short story. Place the answers as they apply to the selection under each question flap before distributing to students, or students can answer the questions themselves.

Resolution

Genre

How was the conflict in this selection resolved?

Describe the main setting in this selection.

Resolution

Setting

Setting

Point of View

What genre of literature is this selection?

From whose point of view is this story told?

Genre

Point of View

Climax

Protagonist

What is the climax of the selection?

Who is the protagonist of the selection?

Climax

Conflict

Conflict

Antagonist

Protagonist

What is the main conflict in the selection?

Who is the antagonist of the selection?

Antagonist

Protagonist

FORTUNE TELLER TEMPLATE

Figurative Language

Students identify examples of figurative language, such as simile, metaphor, alliteration, onomatopoeia, hyperbole, personification, imagery, and symbol.

Metaphor

Alliteration

She is a fish out of water.

Metaphor

Onomatopoeia

Hiss! The snake was ready to attack.

Onomatopoeia

Personification

The sun set slowly.

The telephone pole streched out its arms.

Alliteration

Imagery

Personification

Hyperbole

Her velvety hair cascaded down her sholders.

I studied for the test for a million hours.

Imagery

Simile

Simile

Symbol

A dove with an olive branch.

Symbol

Hyperbole

Her smile is as bright as a light bulb.

FORTUNE TELLER TEMPLATE

Greek and Latin Root Words 1

Students review the Greek and Latin root words *pseudo, ped, scrib, tele, chrono, bene, phys,* and *tact.* Students can create other fortune tellers with different root words.

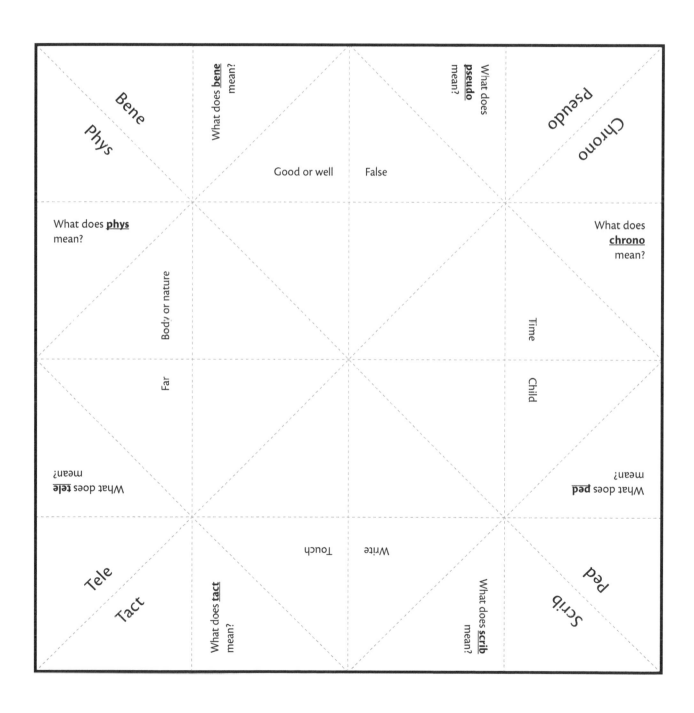

FORTUNE TELLER TEMPLATE

Greek and Latin Root Words 2

Students review the Greek and Latin root words *tract*, *spect*, *vid*, *aud*, *dict*, *port*, *rupt*, and *cede*. Students can create other fortune tellers with different root words.

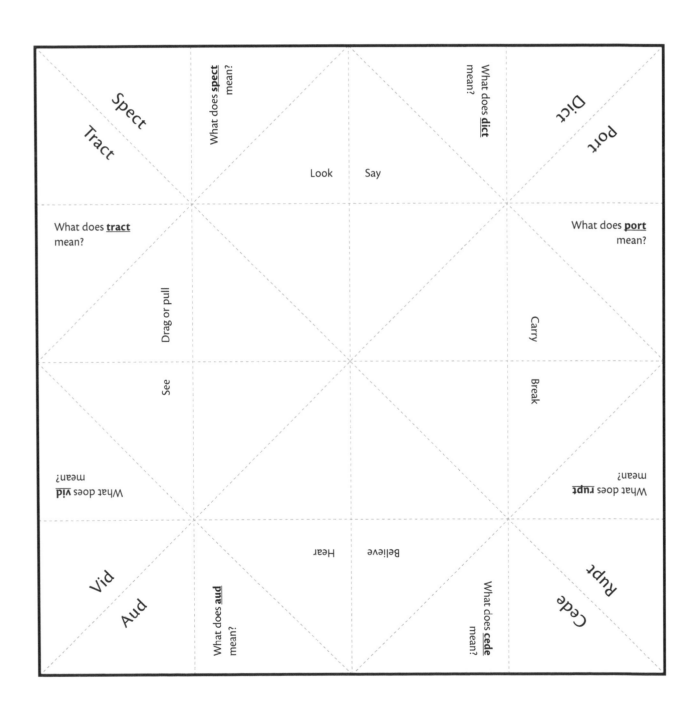

FORTUNE TELLER TEMPLATE

Math Vocabulary

This fortune teller contains sixth-grade math concepts. Teachers in other grades can use this as a model to allow students to create their own fortune tellers that use grade-level concepts.

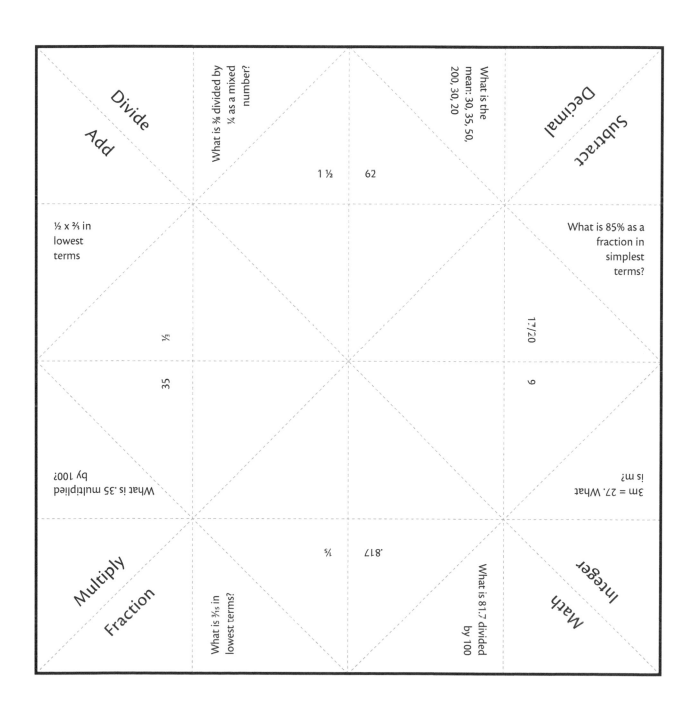

FORTUNE TELLER TEMPLATE

Parts of Speech

Students practice the parts of speech by locating a particular part of speech found in a sentence on the fortune teller.

Noun

Interjection

(tell the noun)
The fish flew out
of the water.

(tell the verb)
Let's fish this
afternoon.

Verb

Pronoun

The **fish** flew
out of the water.

Let's **fish**
this afternoon.

(tell the interjection)
Wow! The sunset
over the water
was a sight
to see.

(tell the pronoun)
Shamu was the
largest whale.
He was
huge!

Shamu was the largest
whale. **He** was huge!

Wow! The
sunset over the water
was a sight to see.

The colorful
fish darted **quickly**
through the water.

The whales migrated,
and their babies followed.

(tell the adverb)
The colorful fish
darted quickly
through the
water.

(tell the conjunction)
The whales
migrated, and
their babies
followed.

Adverb

Adjective

Colorful fish
were all over the reef.

The fish swam all
around the swimmers.

(tell the preposition)
The fish swam all
around the
swimmers.

Preposition

Conjunction

(tell the adjective)
Colorful fish were
all over the
reef.

FORTUNE TELLER TEMPLATE

Prefixes 1

Students review the prefixes *circum-*, *dis-*, *in-*, *mis-*, *post-*, *re-*, *sub-*, and *trans-* and respond to questions that include words with these prefixes. Students can create other fortune tellers with different prefixes.

Mis-

Sub-

Why might you <u>misunderstand</u> what someone tells you?

When would you take a <u>posttest</u>?

Post-

Re-

They are not clear; you do not listen.

After a unit of study.

Do you work above or below the boss if you are a <u>subordinate</u>?

What do you do when you <u>reset</u> your clock?

Below.

Turn it back.

You do not pass; you get poor grades.

You might have an accident. You might get a ticket.

What usually happens when all of your schoolwork is <u>incomplete</u>?

What might happen if you <u>disregard</u> a stop sign?

The distance around the circle.

Take it across a distance.

In-

Circum-

Define the <u>circumference</u> of a circle.

What do you do when you <u>transport</u> something?

Trans-

Dis-

FORTUNE TELLER TEMPLATE

Prefixes 2

Students review the prefixes *anti-, com-, de-, ex-, inter-, intra-, pre-,* and *un-* and respond to questions that include words with these prefixes. Students can create other fortune tellers with different prefixes.

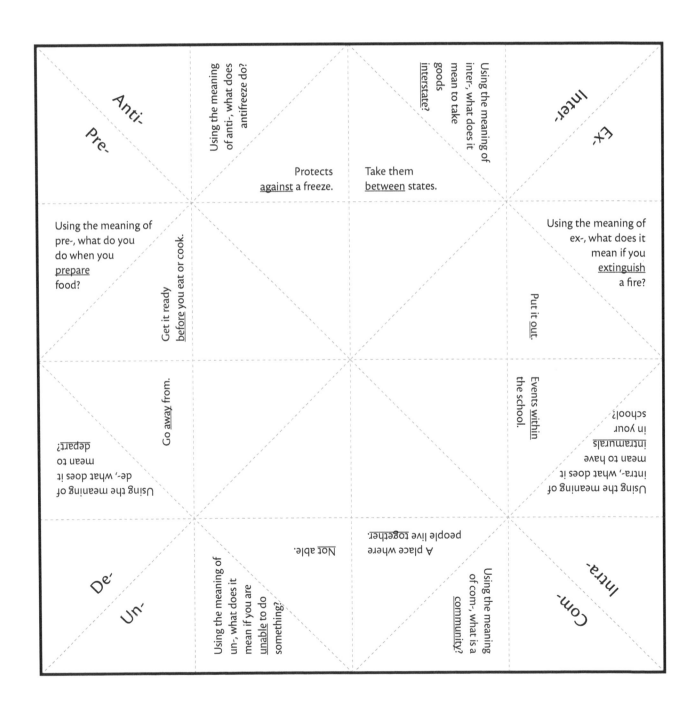

FORTUNE TELLER TEMPLATE

Punctuation

Students practice inserting various types of punctuation into the sentences in the fortune teller.

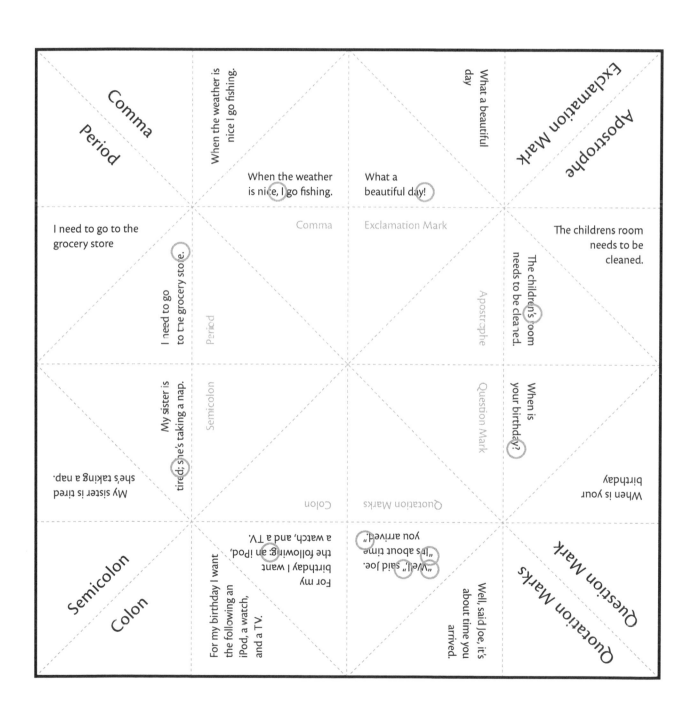

FORTUNE TELLER TEMPLATE

Suffixes 1

Students review the suffixes -able, -ar, -ation, -dom, -ist, -ly, -or, and -sect, and define the suffix they select. Students can create other fortune tellers with different suffixes.

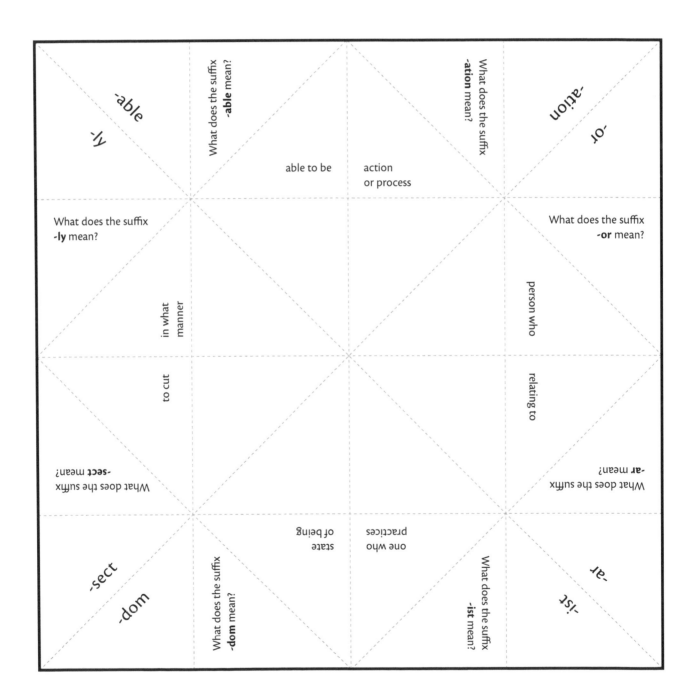

FORTUNE TELLER TEMPLATE

Suffixes 2

Students review the suffixes *-arium, -er, -est, -cle, -less, -ling, -ness,* and *-sion/-tion.* Students determine the suffix definition by defining a word that uses that suffix. Students can create other fortune tellers with different suffixes.

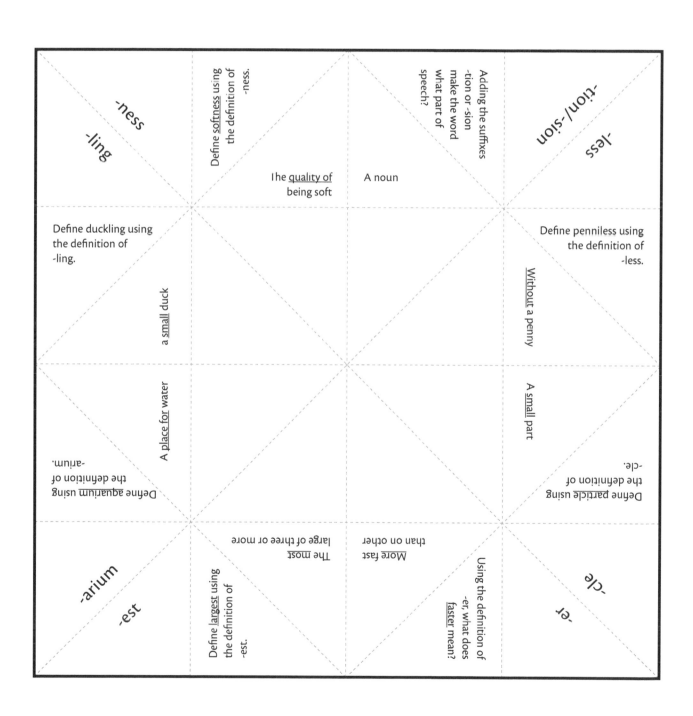

Correlation to the Common Core and Academic Application

The Common Core Standards for each area: reading for literature and informational text, writing, language, and speaking and listening focus on the same concepts, yet the standards increase with rigor throughout each grade level. Thus, Standard 1 for literature focuses on the same concept throughout each grade level but increases in complexity at each grade level.

The standards focus on results rather than means, therefore teachers have the freedom to provide students with the tools and knowledge their professional judgment and experience deem necessary to assist students in meeting the goals set forth in the standards (Common Core Standards, 2010). Text complexity is an integral component of the Common Core Standards. It is a teacher's job to ensure that students leave one grade level prepared to be successful at the next grade level.

All the academic activities in *Student Engagement is FUNdamental* support the goals of the Common Core Standards. On the following pages, you will find correlation charts showing which standards can be addressed when using the various activities. Depending on how you decide to implement each project will determine the extent to which standards are addressed. You can choose to address one or several standards for each activity you implement to engage your students.

CROSS-INDEXES OF ACTIVITIES BY ACADEMIC APPLICATION

ACTIVITIES	Concept review	Extended thinking	Figurative language	Listening and speaking	Literary elements	Reading strategies	Research	Vocabulary	Writing
A to Z: All About Me	x					x			
A Novel: Chapter by Chapter					x	x			
Academic Songs or Raps				x	x				x
Active Concept Review	x							x	
And the Winner Is....				x	x		x		x
Applying Reading Strategies						x			
Are You Annoyed?					x				
Before/During/After Reading Strategies	x					x			x
One Word, Many Cognitive Levels		x						x	
Character Connections						x			x
Chunking the Text					x	x		x	x
Cognitive Levels Flip Book	x	x							x
Collage of Self					x		x		x
Create a Character		x			x				x
Create a Symbol		x	x		x				x
Extended Thinking		x			x				
Fiction Frenzy					x				
Figurative Language Scavenger Hunt			x						
Figurative Language			x						

CROSS-INDEXES OF ACTIVITIES BY ACADEMIC APPLICATION

ACTIVITIES	Concept review	Extended thinking	Figurative language	Listening and speaking	Literary elements	Reading strategies	Research	Vocabulary	Writing
Getting to Know You				X	X		X		X
Give One/Get One Flip Book	X	X		X	X	X	X		
Graffiti Wall	X								
Greek and Latin Root Words								X	
Math Vocabulary	X							X	
Me Bags or Boxes	X			X	X				
Interactive Bookmark					X	X		X	X
Introductory Elements									X
Literary Analysis					X				
Parts of speech	X								
Personal Website Poster					X		X		X
Podcasting		X		X	X		X		X
Prefixes								X	
Punctuation	X								X
Reading Comprehension						X			
Rhetorical Rally	X			X					
Self Pop-Up			X						X
Step by Step	X								X
Student Directory					X		X		X

CROSS-INDEXES OF ACTIVITIES BY ACADEMIC APPLICATION

ACTIVITIES	Concept review	Extended thinking	Figurative language	Listening and speaking	Literary elements	Reading strategies	Research	Vocabulary	Writing
Suffixes								X	
Think-Pair-Share with a Movie		X		X	X				
Thread Twirl	X			X	X				
Tic-Tac-Toe Facts	X				X			X	
To Know Me is to Love Me	X		X		X	X		X	
To Tell the Truth	X			X	X		X	X	
Two-Column Notes					X	X			
Vocabulary Connections								X	
Vocabulary Poetry								X	X
Web Quest Challenge							X		
Who Said It?		X			X				X
Writing on the Wall		X			X	X			X

Activity	S&L 1	S&L 2	S&L 3	S&L 4	S&L 5	S&L 6	S&L 7	S&L 8	S&L 9	S&L 10	Lit 1	Lit 2	Lit 3	Lit 4	Lit 5	Lit 6	Lit 7	Lit 8	Lit 9	Lit 10
Writing on the Wall																				
Who Said It?											X	X	X			X	X			X
Web Quest Challenge	X										X	X	X			X	X			X
Vocabulary Poetry												X	X							X
Vocabulary Connections														X						
Two-Column Notes														X						
To Tell the Truth											X	X	X	X		X	X		X	X
To Know Me is to Love Me											X	X	X	X		X				X
Tic-Tac-Toe Facts											X	X	X							X
Thread Twirl											X	X	X	X	X	X				X
Think-Pair-Share with a Movie	X	X		X		X					X	X	X			X	X			
Student Directory	X	X	X	X																
Step by Step											X	X								
Self Pop-Up											X		X							
Rhetorical Rally											X	X	X	X		X				X
Podcasting	X	X	X	X							X	X	X			X				
Personal Website Poster	X	X	X	X	X	X					X	X	X			X	X			X
Interactive Bookmark											X	X	X							X
Me Bags or Boxes	X										X	X	X	X	X	X	X		X	X
Graffiti Wall	X	X	X	X	X	X					X	X	X							X
Give One/Get One Flip Book											X	X	X	X	X	X	X		X	X
Getting to Know You											X	X	X	X		X			X	X
Create a Symbol	X	X	X	X	X	X					X	X	X							
Create a Character											X	X	X							X
Collage of Self											X		X			X				
Cognitive Levels Flip Book	X										X	X	X							X
Chunking the Text											X	X	X			X	X		X	X
Character Connections											X	X	X	X		X				X
Are You Annoyed?													X			X				
And the Winner is....	X			X							X		X			X				X
Active Concept Review	X	X	X	X	X	X					X	X	X							X
Academic Songs or Raps														X						X
A to Z: All About Me	X	X		X		X					X	X	X							X
Standards	X													X						X

INFORMATIONAL TEXT: 1 2 3 4 5 6 7 8 9 10

LANGUAGE: 1 2 3 4 5 6

Beck, Isabel, Margaret McKeown, and Linda Kucan. *Bringing Words to Life:Robust Vocabulary Instruction*. New York: Guilford Press, 2002.

Bradbury, Ray. "The Drummer Boy of Shiloh." In *Prentice Hall Literature, Grade 8*. ew Jersey: Pearson, 2010.

Chopin, Kate. "The Story of an Hour." Accessed September 12, 2011. http://www.pbs.org/katechopin/library/storyofanhour.html.

Cleary, Brian P. *Hairy, Scary, Ordinary: What Is an Adjective?* Illustrated by Jenya Prosmitsky. Carolrhoda Books, 2001.

Cleary, Brian P. *A Mink, A Fink, A Skating Rink: What Is a Noun?* Illustrated by Jenya Prosmitsky. Lerner Publishing Group, 1999.

Cleary, Brian P. *To Root, to Toot, to Parachute: What Is a Verb?* Illustrated by Jenya Promitsky. Carolrhoda Books, 2001.

Cleary, Brian P. *Dearly, Nearly, Insincerely: What Is an Adverb?* Illustrated by Brian Gable. First Avenue Editions, 2005.

Cleary, Brian P. *Under, Over, By the Clover: What Is a Preposition?* Illustrated by Brian Gable. Millbrook Press, 2003.

National Governors Association Center for Best Practices and Council of Chief State School Officers. "Common Core Standards." Accessed September 12, 2011.http://www.corestandards.org/the-standards.

Dale, Edgar. *Audio-Visual Methods in Teaching*, 43. New York: Dryden Press, 1956.

Dean, Nancy. *Voice Lessons: Classroom Activities to Teach Diction, Detail, Imagery, Syntax, and Tone*. Gainesville, Fl.: Maupin House, 2000.

Feber, Jane. *Active Word Play*. Gainesville, Fl.: Maupin House, 2008.

Feber, Jane. *Creative Book Reports*. Gainesville, Fl.: Maupin House, 2004.

Freedman, Russell. "A Backwoods Boy." In *Prentice Hall Literature, Grade 6*. New Jersey: Pearson, 2010.

Galdone, Paul. *The Three Little Pigs*. New York: Clarion Books, 1970.

Harvey, Stephanie, and Anne Goudvis. *Strategies That Work: Teaching Comprehension to Enhance Understanding*, 68. Maine: Stenhouse, 2000.

Hess, Karin K., Dennis Carlock, Ben Jones, and John R. Walkup. "What exactly do "fewer, clearer, and higher standards" really look like in the classroom? Using a cognitive rigor matrix to analyze curriculum, plan lessons, and implement assessments." Accessed September 12, 2011. www.nciea.org/publications/cognitiverigorpaper_KH11.pdf.

London, Jack. "The King of Mazy May." In *Prentice Hall Literature, Grade 6*. New Jersey: Pearson, 2010.

Lowry, Lois. *Number the Stars*. New York: Yearling, 1990.

Lyons, Carol A., and Gay Su Pinnell. *Systems for Change in Literacy Education: A Guide to Professional Development*. New Hampshire: Heinemann, 2001.

Marzano, Robert J., and Jana S. Marzano. "The Key to Classroom Management." *Educational Leadership* 61, No. 1. Accessed September 12, 2011. http://www.ascd.org/publications/educationalleadership/sept03/vol61/num01/abstract.aspx.

Meyer, Stephenie. *Twilight*. New York: Little, Brown and Co., 2005.

Meyer, Stephenie. *Eclipse*. New York: Little, Brown and Co., 2007.

Overbaugh, Richard C. & Lynn Schultz. "Bloom's Taxonomy." Accessed September 12, 2011. http://www.odu.edu/educ/roverbau/Bloom/blooms_taxonomy.htm.

Philbrick, Rodman. *Freak the Mighty*. New York: Scholastic, 2001.

Rasinski, Timothy V. *The Fluent Reader: Oral Reading Strategies for Building Word Recognition, Fluency, and Comprehension*, 23. New York: Scholastic, 2003.

Rupley, William H., John W. Logan, and William D. Nichols. "Vocabulary instruction in a balanced reading program." The Reading Teacher 52 (1998/1999): 338/6-346.

Sachar, Louis. *Holes*. New York: Yearling, 2000.

Stipek, Deborah. "Relationships Matter." *Educational Leadership* 64, No.1. Accessed September 12, 2011. http://www.ascd.org/publications/educational-leadership/sept06/vol64/num01/Relationships-Matter.aspx.

Shusterman, Neal. *Everlost*. New York: Simon & Schuster, 2006.

Steinbeck, John. *The Pearl*. New York: Bantam Books, 1963.

Zemelman, Steven, Harvey Daniels, and Arthur Hyde. *Best Practice: New Standards for Teaching and Learning in America's Schools*. New Hampshire: Heinemann. 1998.